ISLAMIC AFRICA

ISLAMIC AFRICA
Incorporating SUDANIC AFRICA

Contents

BOOK REVIEWS

Islamic Africa is a peer-reviewed, multidisciplinary, academic journal published by Northwestern University Press in collaboration with the Institute for the Study of Islamic Thought in Africa (ISITA), based at Northwestern University, Evanston. The journal incorporates *Sudanic Africa*, retaining its focus on historical sources, bibliographies, and methodologies. *Islamic Africa* promotes interaction between scholars of Islam and Africa across all continents and across historical periods. We welcome papers on any aspect of Islam and Muslim life pertaining to Africa and/or Africans from the humanities and the social sciences, especially those originating from the African continent.

SOURCES

Muslim Responses to British Colonialism in Northern Nigeria as Expressed in Fulfulde Poems

*Mallam M. Bashir Abubakar,** ADAMAWA STATE UNIVERSITY, MUBI, NIGERIA

DOI: 10.5192/21540993040101

ABSTRACT

The pioneer of Fulfulde poetry in written Arabic/ajami was Shehu Uthmān bin Fodiye, who led a jihad in 1804 for the purification of Islam in Sokoto, northern Nigeria, also known as Hausa Land. His contemporaries followed his footsteps and the poetic tradition of resistance continues to the present day. This article examines poems that are concerned with Muslim responses to British colonial occupation in northern Nigeria, expressed in the Fulfulde language. The poets express that the myth of well-received and accepted colonial occupiers, propagated by the West, was in fact not true. Scholarly support is given to highlight the fierce battles, killings, and destructions of property that finally resulted in the imposition of colonial rule upon the people of northern Nigeria, replacing the more moderate Sokoto Caliphate.

* I would like to thank immensely Dr. Mukhtar Abdullahi Bunza of the Department of History, Usmanu Danfodiyo University, Sokoto, Nigeria, for his great contribution towards the fulfillment of this article. Dr. Bunza has offered me numerous materials for reference, without which this article would not have been rich enough to this standard. Special thanks go to Dr. Alkasum Abba, the Vice Chancellor of Adamawa State University, Mubi, Nigeria, who gave me attention in answering my questions regarding the historical facts of Bokki Hampeeto and the general history of Yola town. He also encouraged me to translate my Fulfulde poems into English for wider reach. I am also indebted to my sons Hamid Bashir and Aliyu Bashir for helping me type the entire article.

Islamic Africa, VOL. 4, NO. 1, 2013. ISSN 2154-0993.

The following poems are a set of three compositions concerned with Muslim responses to British colonialism in northern Nigeria as expressed in Fulfulde verse. Fulfulde is the language of a people who call themselves Fulɓe (plural of Pullo), sometimes also known as Fulani in Nigeria. Fulfulde is spoken in twenty-three countries in Africa, making it one of the most widely dispersed languages on the continent. Fulfulde (the language) and Fulɓe (the people) go hand in hand with Pulfule, the dialect, and Pulaaku, the culture in which poetry is a primary mode of public and personal expression.

The tradition of Fulfulde verse is one that likely stretches back centuries as an oral genre. Its written form, however, is of much more recent vintage. Prior to the imposition of British colonial rule at the end of the nineteenth century, northern Nigeria was governed by the Sokoto Caliphate. The founder of the Caliphate, Shehu Uthmān bin Fodiye (1754–1817), was a religious revivalist, a social reformer, and a political innovator. However, he was also a poet. The Shehu was the pioneer of Fulfulde poetry in its written form, composing an incredibly large corpus of poems throughout his lifetime. The works composed by him and his followers were, for the most part, spiritually didactic in nature. Through a synthesis of Fulfulde and Arabic poetic form, Shehu Uthmān, his son Muhammad Bello (d. 1837), and his daughter Nana Asma'u (d. 1864) produced vast collections of verse aimed at instructing their fellow believers on topics such as correct belief and practice, proper social conduct, and the shape of the cosmos. Though produced in written form, they were widely disseminated throughout Fulɓe society through already existing oral networks of transmission. As a result, the Shehu's innovative verse, which owed a great deal to classical Arabic/Islamic forms, spread widely throughout Fulfulde poetic circles, and ultimately created a new literary paradigm whose influence would be felt well into the twentieth century.

Written Fulfulde poetry was first introduced by Shehu Uthmān as a way of communicating his vision to a largely nonliterate public. His aim was not simply to mobilize the people to join and support the jihad, but to provide them with a foundation of proper Islamic doctrine that could serve as a basis for their actions. One possible solution was to compose religious texts in local languages instead of Arabic, which was the norm until then. However, the use of the indigenous languages for the production of religious tracts alone could not surmount the problem of transmitting ideas to the community at large in what was a predominantly oral society. Shehu, therefore, resorted to poetry. Verse was a genre with a long history of oral transmission that could easily be turned to didactic uses. It should come as little surprise that it was enormously effective in reaching and capturing the hearts of his audience.[1]

The verse of the Shehu was almost exclusively religious in nature. The poems presented here, however, take a somewhat more secular bent and constitute the response of Fulfulde poets to British conquest. The three selections are from a collection I have termed "Faggo Maama," which simply means "assorted items," reflecting the variety of poems it contains. However, they are all concerned with the travails of colonial rule. Collectively, these poems provide interesting portraits of various aspects of British colonial rule, including the poets' impression of the British conquerors; the consequences of territorial reorganization that ignored patterns of precolonial boundaries, habitation, and social relations; and the disruption of the economic, political, social, and cultural systems of the caliphate. As we will see below, while dealing primarily with the profane, these verses are not devoid of allusions to the sacred with frequent references to God, the Qur'an, and the use of stock Islamic motifs such as "*munafiqun*" or "hypocrites," all of which reaffirm the centrality of the faith in Fulfulde literature.

The poems are:

1. "Garol Nasaara"—"The Coming of the White Man." The word *Nasaara* here refers to Europeans, as opposed to its original usage in the Holy Qur'an referring to Christians. The poem is part of a larger work composed by Malam Hamaseyo Girei, a popular poet in Adamawa State of Nigeria. He probably wrote the poem in the 1920s, and it consists of twenty-four dual-stanza lines or verses. The theme of the poem seeks to convey the historical facts of how the British came to Yola in September 1901 and used force to take control of the emirate.

2. "Keeri Dow Hawa"—"The Artificial Boundaries." This poem was composed by Malam Buba Jarida, who used to also draw images of people and to comment on them, rather than writing poems. It was not dated but mostly corresponds to the process of territorial reorganization by Britain and France, which was well under way by 1918 (when Germany was conquered in World War I). The theme of the poem focuses on the disruption caused by the creation

[1] For a more complete discussion of the evolution of Fulfulde poetry during the period of the Sokoto Caliphate, see Beverly B. Mack and Jean Boyd, *One Woman's Jihad: Nana Asma'u, Scholar and Scribe* (Bloomington: Indiana University Press, 2000).

of formal borders during the colonial period, which affected the lives of those living between Nigeria and Cameroon.

3. "Heeferɓe Njabtii Ardungal"—"The Unbelievers Snatched the Leadership." This poem is believed to have been written by Malam Hammadu Mo Bindi, a disciple of Malam Muhammad Tukur ɓii Binta. Malam Tukur wrote many poems, and one of the most popular among them is a voluminous work titled *Busra'u*, containing well over one thousand verses of dual-stanza lines. The eighteen dual-stanza lines included here are believed to be part of a longer poem containing forty dual-stanza lines, which dates from about 1915. The theme of these lines focuses on memories of the good governance of the Sokoto Caliphate in northern Nigeria, which was destroyed by the British.

In the following pages, the selected poems are presented with each line of the Fulfulde version followed by the English translation. Annotations are provided for additional explanation of motifs, historical facts, and additional context.

POEM 1

GAROL NASAARA
THE COMING OF THE WHITE MAN

1.1 Garki Nasaara laatake dow fomnde,
1.2 Ngoo Biniwoy ngo roondi ɓurɗum ɓolde.
The coming of the White Man was by the river,
This very Benue River carried sophisticated ammunition.
2.1 Naafikiʾen hoɓɓe ɓe ɗaɓɓay beero,
2.2 To fomnde mayo ton ɓe weeri naa wuro.
The visitors[2] who were hypocrites did not look for a host,
It was at the riverside that they resided, not in town.
3.1 Werde nde maɓɓe laati laana maɓɓe,
3.2 Ton ɓe hoɗii e balmi kaɓɓe kaɓɓe.
Their hosting place was their ship,
They resided there with heaps of ammunition.
4.1 Ballo Mo maɓɓe teema Hamman Peeto,
4.2 Ga Lekki ɓokki jammoraa Hampeeto.

[2] Those whose mission was negative on the community did not want to come out clearly.

Their aid[3] might be one called Hampeeto,
Because the Baobab Tree[4] was nicknamed Hampeeto.

5.1 Ɓokki ki Hampeeto fu seedi garki,
5.2 Nganam to ɓakki maaki laanawal faki.
Even the Baobab Tree of Hampeeto[5] witnessed the coming,
Because it was near it that the ship got anchored.

6.1 Ki eewi ɓaade laamu maati diggi,
6.2 Ɗi bundugaaru tawma yonki eggi.
It could scan the royal house[6] confused with chaos,
That of a gun, hoping that those around escaped.

7.1 Kaawu mo am wiʾii ɓe tamma darngal,
7.2 Nyannde nde'e ɓe ngi ko ɓarti ɓargal.
My maternal uncle said they thought it was a doomsday,
That very day they saw something more than Power.[7]

8.1 Anndi Zubairu Kam to heedi saaʾi nden,
8.2 Ɓe ndulli toy O heedi fuuna nyannde nden.
Oh! Whereabout of Zubairu[8] [the emir] at that time,
His whereabouts was a mystery on that day.

9.1 Biiɗo ma yii mo fu o ɓaddinaama,
9.2 He fewre sei o hun o hunniraama.
Anyone who told you that he had seen him,[9] what he said was,
Near to telling a lie, unless he swore and made to swear.

---

[3] People believed that a man called Hamman Peeto climbed one baobab tree found (maybe on his farm) there to point to the British troops where the emir's (Lamiɗo's) palace was. It was from the top of that tree they fired on the palace and the Central Mosque.

[4] Otherwise known as monkey bread tree, or botanically *Adansonia digitata*, this was a tree near the bank of the Benue River, where the British ship was anchored. This was on September 2, 1901 (Alkasum Abba). Dr. Alkasum Abba of the history department of Ahmadu Bello University, Zaria, Nigeria, was interviewed by me in February 2012.

[5] With reference to note 3 above, the baobab tree was referred to in history as "Ɓokki Hampeeto," or the Baobab Tree of Hampeeto.

[6] From the top of Hampeeto's tree one could scan the outbreak of fire and people scattered in confusion.

[7] People thought that their emir (Lamiɗo) was the ultimate and sole power, and suddenly one day they witnessed such an unthinkable event.

[8] Lamiɗo Zubairu was the emir at that time. He resisted the imposition of colonial rule and fought a guerilla war against the British for nearly two years.

[9] Lamiɗo Zubairu's exit was a mystery to many people, and as such whoever said he had seen him must also prove it and be asked to lead the White Man to get him dead or alive.

10.1 Deftere Allah mawnde teddinaande,
10.2 Nden bo ni wattam 'yamɗe heewan kaade.
By the holy book of Allah,
And even so, he would be subjected to tough interrogation.[10]
11.1 Lamɗo Zubairu calɗo keefaraaku,
11.2 O majjiti o dilli marɗo risku.
Lamiɗo [Emir] Zubairu could not be a party to unbelief,
He vanished and left honorably.
12.1 Woɓɓe mbiʾi o jooɗa ɗum laruura,
12.2 O wii ɓe defte Allah ɓur basiira.
Some said he should stay due to necessity,[11]
He said to them that holy books spoke with clarity.
13.1 O ɓesdoyaayi ɗon o haaɗi kul ma.
13.2 Woɓɓe ni ɓesdanii mo marɓe himma.
He did not add anything to what he said, but,
Some who knew *what he meant*[12] extended.
14.1 Annduɓe Kaɓɓe deftere nde Allah,
14.2 Ɓe tokkini hadiise Bajjo Allah.
Those who knew where to quote from Allah's book,
And also followed by narrating the traditions of Allah's Prophet.
15.1 Omoto le ngol Awfu ngi'aa aayaaje,
15.2 Tatiije tokkindirɗe fahmu haaje.
Open Chapter 5 of Awf and refer to verses,[13]
The three verses, near one another, and understand your needs.
16.1 Ɓe'en ɓe hiitoraaki ɗum ko jibbina,
16.2 Wi'aama kamɓe ɓen ɓe kaafiruuna.
Those who fail to abide by what has been revealed,[14]
It is said that they are [the same as] unbelievers.

---

[10] At the hands of British troops, in order to find Lamiɗo Zubairu.

[11] Some scholars (such as Alkali Hamajoɗa) advised Lamiɗo Zubairu to stay, but he refused, saying that to his understanding it was an abomination to allow unbelievers to come and destroy the religion of God.

[12] Zubairu refers here to verses of the Holy Qurʾan.

[13] Parts of verses 44, 45, and 47 of the Qurʾan state as follows: (i) . . . And whoever doesn't judge by what God has revealed, then it is those who are the disbelievers. (ii) . . . And whoever doesn't judge by what God has revealed, then it is those who are the wrongdoers (unjust). (iii) . . . And whoever doesn't judge by what God has revealed, then it is those who are the defiantly disobedient.

[14] See note 13 (i) above.

17.1 Ɓe'en ɓe hiitoraaki ɗum ko jibbina,
17.2 Wi'aama kamɓe ɓen ɓe zaalimuuna.
Those who fail to abide by what has been revealed,[15]
It is said that they are [the same as] wrongdoers.
18.1 Ɓe'en ɓe hiitoraaki ɗum ko jibbina,
18.2 Wi'aama kamɓe ɓen ɓe faasiƙuuna.
Those who fail to abide by what has been revealed,[16]
It is said that they are [the same as] hypocrites.
19.1 Allah Ceniiɗo ngecci'en nder aaya,
19.2 Walaa Ko yelditen calen ɗum daaya.
Allah, the exalted told us in the verses [of Qurʾan],
So we have no reason [whatsoever] to refuse, lest it be out of control.[17]
20.1 Zubairu sappi sappoyaaki Boobo,
20.2 No laati fu Nasaara Sufti Bobbo.
Whether Lamido Zubairu showed a sign that Bobbo should take over or not,
Bobbo[18] was the choice of the White Man.
21.1 Ko ɓawtini ɓaawo ɓe wayli laamu,
21.2 Koo ɗume sei biiɗe Nasaara fahmu.
From there on, the leadership changed,
Everything became what the White Man said.
22.1 Ba ɗum waɗaa nanmi e gelle goɗɗe,
22.2 Ko famtinaami haa e mawɗe goɗɗe.
Something of this nature happened elsewhere in other towns too,[19]
I was made to understand, that even the bigger cities experienced it.
23.1 Sokkoto anndu berniwol ngol Sheehu,
23.2 Gwandu yo martaba Kano e caahu.
As you are aware, Sokoto was the seat of the sheikh,
Gwandu was righteous one and Kano was generous.
24.1 Ɗe'ee fu yiidoyii e camngal sheeɗan,
24.2 Ko lutti banda moltoyaaki sheeɗan.
All these [cities] were not free from the devilish act,
What else [do we do] apart from taking refuge (with Allah).

[15] See note 13 (ii) above.
[16] See note 13 (iii) above.
[17] Unless we are overpowered and we have no alternatives, we should continue to struggle.
[18] According to Dr. Alkasum Abba, when Bobbo Ahmadu, Lamiɗo Zubairu's brother, followed him, Zubairu told him to go back and expect to become emir. He was, in fact, appointed emir of Adamawa by the British on September 8, 1901.
[19] Referring to places like Sokoto, Kano, Borno, and elsewhere in the north.

POEM 2

KEERI DOW HAWA
THE ARTIFICIAL BOUNDARIES

1.1 Ko nanmi maamiraawo oora warta,
1.2 Njayri e feesi jaanyoyaa a hirta.
I heard that my grandfather used to take cattle to pasture in the vast land,
And return with cattle [in the evening] and have supper.
2.1 Nasaara'en faransa sangi tayre,
2.2 Ingila hawtanii ɓe hoosi tayre.
The French fenced one part,[20]
And the British did the same.[21]
3.1 Ɓe mbii e walde maama won yo feere,
3.2 E ton to ooretee bo lesdi feere.
They claimed that where my grandfather was living with his cattle became a different country,[22]
And the pastureland where he used to take his cattle for pasture also became a different country.[23]
4.1 Keeri mbaɗaama ton hawaa'u henndu,
4.2 Ɓillana oora jaanya'en e haddu.
Imaginary divisions were created in the air,
Just to create difficulties for the cattle-herders.
5.1 Almaniʾen fu tamnduno nokkuure,
5.2 Nden daga ɓaawo sammoyii saawabre.
The Germans too claimed a certain portion,
Later on left and abandoned it.
6.1 Almani'en Faransaʾen Biraati,
6.2 Ɓe amtoyii e lesdi ndi ko ɓawti.
The Germans, the French, and the British,
They caused atrocities on this land before.
7.1 Ɓe laaɓa ɓandu amma saani nyiddi,
7.2 Ko sappi anniyaaji ɗin ɓe ngardi.
Their bodies look white, but their manners look ugly,
This indicated the intention they came with.

[20] Meaning the Cameroon Republic.
[21] Meaning Nigeria.
[22] Where they were living became Nigeria.
[23] Where they used to graze their cattle became the Republic of Cameroon.

A Place at the Table: The Political Integration of Muslims in Kenya, 1963–2007

Mohamed Bakari, FATIH UNIVERSITY, BÜYÜKÇEKMECE, ISTANBUL, TURKEY

DOI: 10.5192/21540993040115

ABSTRACT

Kenyan Muslims are well integrated within the Kenyan political system. This process of political integration gained momentum when President Daniel Arap Moi regained power after the aborted military coup attempt by the Kenya Air Force in August 1982. His increasingly authoritarian rule faced a challenge from the younger generation of politicians who began to challenge his legitimacy because of the loss of basic democratic rights through mass demonstrations and civil disobedience. A new generation of Muslim politicians and activists joined the fray. This new Muslim leadership was the product of social transformations that were ushered in by new educational opportunities that presented themselves immediately after Kenya gained independence. Muslims were able to be integrated gradually within the political system through social mobility and pragmatic policies of Jomo Kenyatta and later through the politics of cronyism and co-option under Moi. With the widening of political space and the new politics of inclusion, Muslims have now been completely integrated within Kenyan society.

This paper was first presented at the International Conference on the Political Economy of Kenya, held at St. Anthony's College, Oxford University, May 27–28, 2004. The author is grateful for assistance provided by the Oxford Centre for Islamic Studies and the Ford Foundation during his appointment there as a visiting African Fellow.

Islamic Africa, VOL. 4, NO. 1, 2013. ISSN 2154-0993.

The 1990s was one of the most crucial decades in Kenya's political history. This period was as momentous as the 1960s, which saw the dismantling of British colonialism and the rise of African nationalism. 1992 was a landmark year that heralded in what many people described as "The Second Liberation," where the Moi regime had been challenged by a combination of disparate political forces whose only common ground was their united opposition to his regime's increasingly repressive measures and his personal, autocratic rule. Political activists of all stripes, from Muslim and Christian fundamentalists to Kikuyu underground opposition movements to nonaffiliated political reformers, were determined to dislodge Moi from political power.

At the international level political configurations were also altered by the dismantling of the Soviet Union and the apartheid system in South Africa. The International Monetary Fund and the World Bank were tying the provision of aid and loans, on which the Moi government subsisted, to better human rights records. It was a very inauspicious period for regimes like those built around the cult of the "Big Man." All these voices forced Moi to read the writing on the wall and concede, through a little bit of arm twisting by the international community, to understand the situation and take corrective measures to survive for another two terms. He had already dominated Kenyan politics for the previous unhappy fourteen years, which included an abortive coup attempt[1] and several political murders. But the defining characteristic, in the perception of the general public both at home and abroad, was Moi's unalloyed corruption. It must also be said that corruption, as a national way of life, was not unique to the Moi regime. The African continent was replete with regimes of such corruption that Moi's was just one that seemed to stand out. The culture of corruption in Africa was instrumental in Africa's lack of political and economic progress. A significant body of literature has addressed this African incubus, for example in Jean-Francois Bayart's *The State in Africa: The Politics of the Belly* (1993), *Africa Works: Disorder as a Political Instrument* (1999) by Jean-Pascal Daloz and Patrick Chabal, and Pierre Englebert's *State Legitimacy and Development* (2002), all of which try to grapple with the factors that have contributed to persistent African underdevelopment. Moi was singularly responsible for the manipulation of state institutions in

---

[1] See Godwin R. Muraunga, "The State, Reforms and the Question of Legitimacy in Kenya," *Identity, Culture and Politics* 5, nos. 1–2 (2004): 179–206.

order to plunder national resources and ensure the survival of his regime through the misuse of these resources to bribe opponents and detractors into compromise. One of the most infamous corruption scandals from the Moi era is the Ponzi scheme that has come to be known as the Goldenberg Affair. In the words of Deremo Maiko, "No single financial event has had a more far-reaching impact on the Kenyan economy than the hydra-headed Goldenberg Scandal of 1990 to 1993. While the amounts that were involved are yet to be determined, Kenyans are still counting the cost."[2] A decade after the Moi regime was voted out in 2002, this scandal is still under investigation. This seemed the proverbial last straw on the camel's back for the overwhelming majority of Kenyans.

Among the oppositional forces to the Moi regime was a significant segment of the Muslim population of Kenya. Paradoxically, Moi cast himself as a Christian president and used public media to cultivate the classic Machiavellian image of a pious politician, employing a public display of religiosity through government media broadcast of his church attendances. The Presidential Press Unit was always in tow wherever he went in order to film and broadcast his public appearances. He was always shown flanked by a familiar retinue of political opportunists and hangers-on. At the same time he made it possible for Muslims to enter public space in an unprecedented way. This, however, did not stop him from occasionally making disparaging remarks about Islam and Muslims. His grudging acceptance of Muslims as an integral part of Kenyan society was forced on him by circumstances beyond his control. A fateful but abortive coup by junior and inexperienced Kenya Air Force officers in August 1982 forced Moi to reconsider his cultivated antipathy towards Muslims and to take a more nuanced attitude towards them. This change of attitude was forced upon him more by default than design.

The Mission Boy Who Became a President

A product of missionary education, Daniel Arap Moi had embraced the Christian missionary prejudice against Muslims, to which many older generation mission-educated Kenyans subscribed to varying degrees. He willfully tried to re-create the Kenyan nation as a Christian nation, subverting its constitutional foundations as a modern secular state with no

[2] http://www.newsfromafrica.org/newsfromafrica/articles/art_1278.htm.

partiality for any religious group. In this he was completely the opposite of the Kenyan founding father, Mzee Jomo Kenyatta, whose public persona was that of a religiously indifferent national leader who embraced all the shades of religion in the Kenyan multiethnic, multicultural, and multireligious society. This may have had something to do with Kenyatta's training in anthropology at the London School of Economics in the 1930s under the noted anthropologist Bronisław Malinowski. Moi displayed the prejudices of a formally undereducated leader. His education, like that of Idi Amin, terminated at primary school and was followed by a short stint at a primary school teachers' training college. Although he may have continued educating himself privately, there has not been any evidence that he undertook any effort to educate himself in a sustained way. This educational inadequacy was compensated for by his nomination to the colonial Legislative Council as an African representative, where he observed at close quarters the dynamics of politics within the context of colonialism. It may be added that this background not only colored his attitude towards Muslims, but also his cynical and anxiety-ridden dealings with intellectuals and educated people in general. In his dealings with Muslims, he seemed more at home with like-minded Muslim politicians of the same educational background. Perhaps this explains his closeness to Shariff Nassir (1926–2005), General Mahmoud Mohammed, and such non-Muslim politicians as Kariuki Chotora and Mulu Mutisya, and during the dying days of his regime, sycophants and opportunists like Aaron Kanyingi, a car mechanic catapulted to the position of a power broker. Moi used his constitutional privilege to nominate both Mulu Mutisya and Kariuki Chotara to Parliament without going through the hassle of contesting an election.[3] According to the Kenyan Constitution, the president was empowered to nominate twelve members of Parliament, and Moi used the opportunity to handpick those he was sure would sing his tune, and both Mutisya and Chotara fit the bill. They were taken from obscurity to the forefront of political action.

Shariff Nassir was Moi's kingpin at the coast. A scion of a wealthy patrician Swahili coastal family that made its fortune through shipping concerns, Nassir used his father's personal wealth in his political career to advance both himself and his political mentors, like Daniel Arap Moi and Ronald Ngala, earlier in his career.[4] A colorful, flamboyant, and

---

[3] See http//:africapress.me/2008/06/08/public-figures-who-made-the-best-of-court-jesting/.

[4] See B. A. Ogot and William R. Ochieng', *Decolonization and Independence in Kenya 1940–1993* (London: James Currey, 1995).

courageous politician with a common touch, he pledged complete loyalty to Moi throughout his long life in Kenyan politics. He was one of the few Kenyan politicians with an extremely high profile and great name recognition. Utterly anti-tribal and nonsectarian, were he better educated he would have had the potential of wide acceptance as a national politician and national leader of the stature of the charismatic Thomas Joseph Mboya and Mwangi Josiah Kariuki. His lack of education was reflected in his absence of a polished style. Extremely articulate in Kiswahili, he lacked English skills to endear himself to the generally well-educated and sophisticated new generation of Kenyan politicians. He became the public face of the ruling Kenyan African National Union (KANU) party's kitchen cabinet, which made unpopular decisions behind closed doors and forced them on the general public. He was for a long time the KANU district chairman in Mombasa, a powerful office to broker power within the KANU political structure. Shariff Nassir's role as a pliant tool in the hands of Moi has been sufficiently noticed to have him immortalized in Ngugi wa Thiong'o's anti-Moi and anti-Big Man politics fictional work *Wizard of the Crow*[5] as one of the unsavory sycophants singing Moi's tune at the cost of national cohesion and political ethics. The character Sikiokuu (Swahili for "big ear") clearly points to Nassir. Sikiokuu undergoes plastic surgery to equip him with ears big enough to pick up any anti-Moi political gossip and pass it on to his political master. Nassir was often a subject of lampooning in the national press, cartoons appearing with greater frequency as his national stature grew. He was a KANU member of Parliament representing Mombasa central, the Mvita constituency, from 1974 to the time of his death in 2005. He was elected through popular vote at the height of his popularity, and through ballot rigging when his popularity started waning at the rise of the unregistered Islamic Party of Kenya.[6]

Both Mulu Mutisya and Kariuki Chotara were the nearest things to Lenin's "useful idiots"; they were used by Moi to garner the reluctant Kamba and Kikuyu votes. Like Shariff Nassir, both had the lowest academic achievement in Kenya's Parliament.[7]

---

[5] Ngugi wa Thiong'o, *Wizard of the Crow* (London: Harvill Secker, 2006), 28, 162–64.

[6] For the rise of the Islamic Party of Kenya, see Arye Oded, "Islamic Extremism in Kenya: The Rise of Sheikh Khalid Balala," *Religion in Africa* 31, no. 4 (1996): 406–15; Arye Oded, *Islam and Politics in Kenya* (Lynne Rienner, 2000).

[7] http//:africapress.me/2008/06/08/public-figures-who—made-the-best-of-court-jesting/.

The 1990s were already beginning to ignite a new generation of political leaders, people who came of age in the 1980s and 1990s through the expansion of educational opportunities. Most of these were, unlike their predecessors, increasingly university educated. What was true of upcountry was also becoming more common at the coast. Because the Kenyan educational system had played an important integration role, the younger politicians from the various ethnic, racial, and religious backgrounds met at the university or other national institutions that molded them into Kenyans rather than giving them parochial ethnic identities, which constrained them from dealing with other groups. Indeed, this generation of politicians was able to recognize several identities as not incompatible with being Kenyan. When the momentum for a mass movement against Moi picked up, it was the alliances of these younger politicians that played a crucial role in undermining the hegemony of KANU. The latter group was increasingly seen as the party of the older generation of politicians who were too set in their ways to effect a change in the way Kenya was run. KANU was the party of plutocrats united in defending their economic interests in a country that had exacerbated and widened socioeconomic disparities. In his characteristic politics of duplicity, Moi was often able to outflank the younger politicians through the delicate use of money and coercion in winning his sworn enemies, as noted earlier. The biggest hitch for the younger crop of politicians was their lack of money. Money had become the major currency for winning political support, and these politicians had an obvious deficit of this essential commodity. National elections, until 2002, were won on the strength of the presence or absence of money. Those who did have it in sufficient quantities were able to garner a measure of support.

Sheikh Khalid Balala, a rising star in the Muslim political firmament, had access to cash from outside the country. He combined his peculiar charisma with financial rewards to win the support of the young Muslim constituency that he was luring. He was such an important political player at the grassroots level that he became a special concern to then Israeli ambassador to Kenya and a close friend of President Daniel Arap Moi, Dr. Arye Oded. The latter kept a close watch on Muslim politics and personalities as part of his diplomatic docket. A Yemeni Jew who migrated to Israel, Oded later specialized in Islam in Uganda. His background in Arabic helped him to study the rise of Islamism among a section of Kenyan Muslims. It was difficult for someone in his position to have a disinterested view of Islamic politics in an important African country. It is in this context that he began to focus on the activities of Khalid Balala, especially in Balala's threat to Shariff Nassir's dominance of Muslim politics.[8]

No longer did Shariff Nassir have a monopoly of political finance to capture both for himself and for Moi the Muslim vote. Muslims were not immune to the national politics of the checkbook as the ultimate tool to win votes.[9] Balala set up the semblance of a political organization by opening up an office and buying a few cars that aided his mobility. Balala was aware, as were a lot of Muslims, that part of Moi's electoral kitty came from the Middle East. Moi had struck up close friendships with some of the Arab rulers in the Middle East with oil money to buy influence. Thus although he adopted an anti-Muslim posture in his public pronouncements, his international dealings with Muslims were unencumbered by his anti-Muslim rhetoric.

His close Kenyan Muslim allies raised campaign funds for him from other sources, like the Middle East. Balala also wanted a piece of the action for himself to build a local base. The Sudanese came in handy, especially with their anger at Moi's clandestine help for the southern Sudanese rebel forces led by General John Garang. They too wanted to put spanners into Moi's works and the opportunity presented itself in the rise of Sheikh Balala. For a while at least, Balala was swimming in money, just as Shariff Nassir had been; long queues began forming outside Balala's headquarters, just as there were at the Mombasa KANU district headquarters. People were now coming to present the usual problems to Balala, which they had been doing to Shariff Nassir since 1974 when he was first elected to the Mvita constituency. They came to seek money for all sorts of genuine and not so genuine reasons: school fees, food, funeral expenses, house rent, transportation, madrasa teachers' salaries, fines, and so on. The personal system of government Moi ran created in the minds of ordinary Kenyans an aura of money-soaked politicians to whom the constituents could go in their hour of need and to whom the politicians could depend in their own hour of need to be re-elected to Parliament.[10]

---

[8] Donal B. Cruise O'Brien, "Coping with the Christians: The Muslim Predicament in Kenya," in *Religion and Politics in East Africa,* ed. Holger Bernt Hansen and Michael Twaddle (London: James Currey, 1995). See also Oded, *Islam and Politics in Kenya.*

[9] See Mohamed Bakari, "Muslims and the Politics of Change in Kenya," in *Islam in Kenya: Proceedings of the National Seminar on Islam in Kenya*, ed. Mohamed Bakari and Saad S. Yahya (Mewa, 1995).

[10] This author witnessed the stream of supplicants who trooped to Shariff Nassir's house in Nairobi and Mombasa when he was in the company of a former member of Parliament

These were the best conditions for the neglect of social, economic, and political institutions and the reason for their subsequent decline. The national coffers were plundered to meet the insatiable needs of the people and in the process to line the pockets of the politicians, senior civil servants, and their hangers-on. It was therefore natural that during every election season, retired and retiring civil servants were in the first ranks of prospective parliamentary candidates. Everyone was sufficiently tainted and compromised so they were unable to cast the first stone. Sheikh Balala used his newfound resources to rabble rouse and give Moi a few sleepless nights. He also took a leaf from Moi's political strategy: he mobilized his own thugs to intimidate his detractors and Moi's financial supporters among the Muslim business community in Mombasa. The businessmen gave in by diverting part of the money that would otherwise have gone to Moi to Sheikh Balala.[11] Balala used a network of mosques whose imams were personally loyal to him as platforms for his political programs. He was made the "spiritual" head of the new Islamic Party of Kenya (IPK).

The Islamic Party of Kenya: Doing Unto Others What They Do Unto You

The Islamic Party of Kenya was set up by younger Kenyan Muslim activists who were capitalizing on the new unfolding scenario in the country; the re-emergence of multiparty politics that had been made possible by the amendment of the infamous Section 2 (A) of the Constitution of Kenya which had made Kenya a de jure one-party state, and that was only made possible by Moi's capitulating to external pressure.[12] The new party provided an avenue for the emerging young generation of Muslim politicians to exercise their political talent, since there was no political space for them in KANU. As young idealists they were disillusioned by what they perceived as corrupt leadership staying in power via the abuse of the Islamic label. Also, the young leadership was broadly drawn not from the traditional recruiting area of the coast but across the broad spectrum of Kenyan

---

for Malindi Central, Abubakar Badawy, when the latter paid visits to Nassir, his brother-in-law, in the 1990s. I also witnessed the same when I visited Sheik Balala in his office in Makadara, Mombasa, when I went to interview him in the mid-1990s.

[11] Personal communication with Khelef Mohammed, a close ally of Sheikh Balala, sometime in 1992.

[12] B. A. Ogot, "Transition from Single-Party to Multiparty Political System 1989–93," in *Decolonization and Independence in Kenya*, ed. B. A. Ogot and William R. Ochieng' (London: James Currey, 1995).

Muslim society, although the party was perceived primarily as a coastal party. The party chairman, Khalifa Mohammed, was from the coast, while the secretary general, Abdulrahman Wandati, was from Butere, then the constituency of the veteran Kenyan politician and gadfly Martin Shikuku (c. 1933-2012). The party also had the tacit support of young Muslim professionals, the most prominent being Taib Ali Taib, the well-known lawyer and successful businessman who later became the mayor of the city of Mombasa. The young politicians calculated that if Muslims could be mobilized to vote en bloc in the constituencies then they could affect the outcome of elections in predictable ways and could thus enhance the bargaining power of Muslims as a group. They figured that should the Islamic Party of Kenya garner popular Muslim support, then they could send their own party members to Parliament by lending support to candidates of other parties in those areas where their own candidates might not fare well, and in turn get the support of other party supporters where they had the strongest showing. This trade-off was seen as the best strategy for a party that was just starting out. As we shall see, this strategy could not be applied in the interim because of the strong resistance from the government to register the Islamic Party. This resistance was justified in the eyes of KANU because the party drew significant support from areas where Muslims were in the majority, like the Kenya coast and the North Eastern Province that abuts Somalia. The Islamic Party strategists knew that the odds were against them, and as long as KANU called the legal shots they did not stand any chance of being registered, but that should not stop them from carrying on the agitation for registration since this was going to keep them in the public eye. Since there was no legal proviso that said an unregistered party could not call itself by the name it wished to be known, they went on as if they were a legally registered party. This period coincided with the general global Islamic revivalism that ushered in the politics of Islamism, or at least a desire to project Islam into public space. Through the efforts of Islamic preachers, most of whom were increasingly drawn from Saudi-trained ulama, Islamic publications, circulation of cassettes of religious sermons, and the general Islamization of way of life, a high Islamic consciousness was consolidated, as it had been happening elsewhere globally. Identical phenomena have been observed elsewhere in the Islamic world. Important studies on the global rise of Islamism that have relevance to Kenya include the work of Olivier Roy, *Globalized Islam*,[13] Charles

[13] Olivier Roy, *Globalized Islam* (Columbia University Press. 2006).

Hirschkind, *Ethical Soundscapes,*[14] and Patrick Gaffney's *The Prophet's Pulpit.*[15] In Kenya itself, Kai Kresse has done a comparable study on the Ramadan lectures of Sheikh Abdilahi Nassir[16] and their impact on young educated Muslims. Sheikh Abdilahi Nassir in the 1980s and 1990s extensively used the Qur'anic commentaries of Sayyid Qutb, the ideologue of the Muslim Brotherhood of Egypt. All these works observe the phenomenon of Islamization through the use of media, the role of preachers in creating a community of believers that end up affecting political behaviour, and the impact of these transformations on the larger society. For example, increased mosque attendance has given rise to new political consciousness, not only among Muslim men, but also among women.[17] Saba Mahmood and Leila Ahmed found intense engagement of women in both Egypt and the United States of America. Muslims were not only striving to live a personal ethical life as individuals, but to also ensure that ethical living pervades the larger society, which of course does not mean that mosque attendance and the turn towards personal religiosity automatically radicalizes Muslim society. It mostly means new players come into the picture, where, for example, the traditional ulama shaped the worldview of their audiences, Muslim communities now tend to be better educated and aware of global trends. In the words of Roy, "Islam is deterritorialized" and young believers educate themselves on religious matters and form their own opinions on religious, social, and political issues. My own earlier observations on the rise of Islamism in East Africa confirms Roy's hypothesis that the rise of Islamism actually leads to more secularization of Muslims.[18]

In the Kenyan context, the increasing Salafization of Kenyan Islam, from its traditionally liberal, tolerant, and syncretic type to one that is visibly radicalized, can be traced ultimately to the influence of Sheikh

---

[14] Charles Hirschkind, *Ethical Soundscapes: Cassette Sermons and Islamic Counterpublics* (Columbia University Press, 2009).

[15] Patrick Gaffney, *The Prophet's Pulpit: Preaching in Contemporary Egypt,* Comparative Studies on Muslim Societies, University of California Press, 1994.

[16] Kai Kresse, *Philosophising in Mombasa: Knowledge, Islam and Intellectual Practice on the Swahili Coast,* International African Library 35 (Edinburgh University Press, 2007).

[17] Leila Ahmed, *A Quiet Revolution: The Veil's Resurgence, from the Middle East to America* (New Haven, Conn.: Yale University Press, 2011); Saba Mahmood, *Politics of Piety: The Islamic Revival and the Feminist Subject* (Princeton University Press, 2005).

[18] Mohamed Bakari, *The Secularization of Kenyan Muslims: From Marginalization to Re-Invention.* Unpublished manuscript.

Aballah Saleh Farsy, the chief kadhi of Kenya from 1968 to 1982.[19] Almost single-handedly, he was able to swing Islamic practice from one of Shafi orthodoxy to Salafist and Wahhabist complexion. The droves of Kenyan graduates of the Islamic University in Medina were the main catalyst that precipitated this process. The ethnic Somalis constituted the largest number of these graduates.[20] Their influence has had far-reaching repercussions in driving Islam into the public sphere and the emergence of activist Islam. Sheikh Farsy was singularly responsible for inspiring these young ulama to go and seek further education in universities in the Middle East. When they came back many played leading roles in their communities in spearheading the reorientation from orthodox to Saudi modernity. The role of the ulama as the vanguard of change has been well documented by Princeton University's Muhammad Qassim Zaman.[21] The new ulama in Kenya played a decisive role in political consciousness-raising. This inevitably led to the politicization of Islam and Islam became the idiom through which Muslim grievances were articulated.[22] It was this context that gave rise to a new type of Muslim leadership. The older generation of leaders was deemed ineffectual and largely self-serving.

This leadership was the generation that saw the ushering in of nationalist politics, and virtually all of them held political office either in the ruling party or in the opposition parties. In his efforts to control various key

---

[19] On Sheikh Abdallah Saleh Farsy, see Roman Loimeier, "Tradition of Reform, Reform of Tradition: Case Studies from Senegal and Zanzibar/Tanzania," in *Diversity and Pluralism in Islam: Historical and Contemporary Discourse Among Muslims*, ed. Zulfikar Hirji (London: I. B. Tauris), 135–64. See also Roman Loimeier, *Between Social Skills and Marketable Skills: The Politics of Islamic Education in 20th-Century Zanzibar* (Leiden: Brill, 2009).

[20] See Mohamed Bakari, "The New Ulama in Kenya," in *Islam in Kenya: Proceedings of the National Seminar on Contemporary Islam in Kenya,* ed. Mohamed Bakari and Saad S. Yahya (Mewa, 1995).

[21] Muhmamad Qassim Zaman, *The Ulama in Contemporary Islam: Custodians of Change* (Princeton, N.J.: Princeton University Press, 2002).

[22] Hassan J. Ndzovu, *Religion and Politics: The Politicization of Islam in Kenya.* Unpublished manuscript. There is also an increasing body of research on various aspects of Kenyan Islamic politics. Also worth looking at regarding the ethnic polarization among Muslims, see the important work of Ahmed Idha Salim, *The Swahili-Speaking Communities of Kenyan Swahili Coast 1895–1965* (Nairobi: East African Publishing House, 1972); Hassan Mwakimako, "The Ulama and the Colonial State in the Protectorate of Kenya: Politics, Ethnicity, and the Jostling for Power: The Evolution of Institutions of Leadership and Kadhiship in Colonial Kenya" (Ph.D. thesis, University of Cape Town, 2003).

constituencies in national politics, like the trade unions and the Christian clergy, Kenyatta encouraged, as we shall see, the formation of central organizations with which he could deal directly as collective entities. It was this strategy that led, early on, to the formation of the Central Organization of Trade Unions and the National Christian Council of Kenya, which then gave Kenyatta access to these key players through their representative organizations. Until then, the only viable Muslim organization was the one set up by the spiritual leader of the Ismaili community, the Agha Khan, the East African Muslim Welfare Society, which was meant to bring some semblance of organization to the Muslim masses. But this was an East Africa-wide organization that was nonsectarian and gathered under its umbrella both Sunnis and Shias.[23] Balala and his organization appeared to fill in the political void and challenge both the older generation leadership and the authoritarian politics of the ruling party. Although Balala and his group were repeatedly denied registration, they did not go underground but challenged the government by holding demonstrations and organizing acts of civil disobedience.

In the eyes of the IPK, the illegal party was KANU itself, whose actions were seen to betray national aspirations for development by the misuse of public funds. In other words, they saw themselves as occupying a much higher moral ground than KANU itself. As a party the Islamic Party of Kenya has remained in the public consciousness even as it lost the enthusiasm of its supporters for a variety of reasons. What marked it off from KANU at the coast was its ability to shut down the city of Mombasa whenever it needed to do so by its use of strong-arm tactics. The author of this strategy was the now-mellowed activist and a commissioner with the Kenya Human Rights Commission, Khelef Mohammed. He worked out that since KANU misused the local law enforcement agencies to intimidate and harass IPK members, it was legitimate for them too to use dirty tricks on a regime whose stock in trade was also the use of dirty tricks. In its heyday IPK could shut down the city of Mombasa,[24] which was the

[23] See François Constantin, "Leadership, Muslim Identities and East African Politics: Tradition, Bureaucratization and Communication," in *Muslim Identity and Social Change in Sub-Saharan Africa*, ed. Louis Brenner (Bloomington: Indiana University Press, 1993), 36–58. See also François Constantin: "The Attempts to Create Muslim National Organizations in Tanzania, Kenya and Uganda," in *Religion and Politics in East Africa,* ed. Holger Bernt Hansen and Michael Twaddle (London: James Currey, 1995), 19–32.

[24] See Oded, *Islam and Politics in Kenya.*

lifeline and one of the mainstays of the Kenyan economy.[25] The country lost millions of shillings when the city shut down for a few days, needless to say adversely affecting its international image. The young IPK activists were fully cognizant of the implications of their strategies. The city was simply shut down by the mere act of sending anonymous intimidation notes to business owners that, should they open on an appointed day, their shops or businesses would be especially targeted for vandalization. In the moral calculus of the IPK activists the presence of routine torture, in especially constructed torture chambers, of political opponents of KANU was enough justification to violently challenge an increasingly discredited regime.

There were several cases of human rights violations documented both by the IPK itself and also by Amnesty International in its annual country profiles.[26] The IPK documented cases to justify its high-handed tactics. A number of their activists were driven into enforced exile in the United Kingdom and Canada, and the trickle of activist outward migration led to the establishment of sizable refugee communities in those countries. Both internally and outside, the IPK activists adopted more sophisticated tactics in their survival strategies. They saw themselves no longer as lone fighters, but as part of the country-wide movement mobilizing to confront and ultimately dislodge the KANU regime. In this regard, they joined forces with both internal anti-Moi forces and those from the outside, and especially among the Kikuyu dissidents who had consistently opposed his rule for over a decade. The Kikuyu saw Moi at the head of a de-Kikuyunization campaign to purge this enterprising and well-educated ethnic group from the corridors of political and economic power. Moi and his associates were determined to undo the entrenchment of this group by Kenyatta and his Kikuyu cronies. It is important to note that in this purging campaign Moi had the tacit support of virtually all the other ethnic groups who wanted to see the Kikuyu political and economic power redressed to create a more equitable socioeconomic and political system, little realizing that this ethnic vendetta could spiral out of control and engulf the repression of individuals from other ethnic groups who thought in more national terms rather than parochial ones. In the exiled Swahili community the Kikuyu found natural allies in the Muslim refugees.[27]

---

[25] Personal communication with Khelef Mohammed, Mombasa, ca. 1992.

[26] http//:amnesty.org/en/library/asset/AFR32/009/1992/en/05f0d987-f93b-11dd-92e7-c59f81373cf2/afr320091992en.pdf.

[27] Personal communication, Abdilatif Abdalla, July 15, 1992, London.

The Kikuyu-Muslim Alliance in Exile

It was the presence in London of Abdilatif Abdalla,[28] a former BBC Swahili language broadcaster, lexicographer, and the poet laureate of the Swahili language, who actually managed to bring together the Muslim anti-Moi and Kikuyu activist forces into a coalition.[29] Abdilatif himself had suffered under the Kenyatta regime, but as a Kenyan nationalist and socialist was capable of distancing the entire Kikuyu tribe from the misdoings of the Kenyatta regime. He preached about guarding against the demonization of an entire ethnic group on the basis of the misrule of a small Kiambu coterie. When still in his late teens, Abdilatif had been "tried" and found "guilty" of sedition in the late 1960s.

He served a five-year jail term at Kamiti's[30] maximum security prison for writing and distributing a pamphlet entitled *Kenya Twendapi?* (*Where Is Kenya Headed to?*) that was deemed seditious under Kenya's draconian sedition laws. This law was to be used often to put under control all those who used the printed word to challenge the KANU regime. Ironically, on his release and eventual relocation to the University of Dar es Salaam's Institute of Kiswahili Research, in 1972, he was to win the prestigious Kenyatta Literature Prize for his prison poems, *Sauti Ya Dhiki* (*The Voice of Agony*). Abdilatif was also a close friend of the celebrated Kenyan novelist, playwright, and postcolonial theorist Professor Ngugi Wa Thiong'o, who had also been driven into exile by the Moi regime after he had been released from political detention in 1978 after Kenyatta died. Abdilatif and Ngugi provided the vital link between the Kenyan Muslim activists and the Kikuyu exiles. Abdilatif was also a close friend of Oginga Odinga (1911–1994) and was in fact the Kenya People's Union's local boss at the coast before he decided to leave the country. He was later to be the linchpin of the opposition political exiles in London and was later to bring the Luo element closer to the Kikuyu by embracing Raila Odinga as part of the national opposition. So, although Abdilatif was not part of the IPK, he encouraged them in their anti-Moi activities at the international level by

---

[28] See Ngugi wa Thiong'o, "Postcolonial Politics and Culture," in *Moving the Centre: The Struggle for Cultural Freedoms* (London: James Currey, 2008).

[29] Personal communication, Abdilatif Abdalla, Leipzig, May 5, 2010.

[30] Abdilatif Abdalla, *Sauti Ya Dhiki* (Nairobi: Oxford University Press, 1973), Preface, xiii. See also Hyder Kindy, *Life and Politics in Mombasa* (Nairobi: East African Publishing House, 1972).

connecting them to other pan-Kenyan activists. Abdilatif also had strong connections with Amnesty International. The attention of the latter organization was drawn to gross violations of the human rights of Muslims in Kenya. The early IPK activists formed an association, the Waswahili Refugee Association, with an address in England. The association was soon issuing a magazine with political content, called *Waswahili Voice*.[31]

Through this medium they documented what they alleged were human rights abuses and disappearances of political activists. The IPK now cut an image of a serious organization and formed informal political alliances internally and provided liaisons in London and Toronto.

There were now sufficiently enough IPK exiles to form a visible group that heckled Moi when he visited London. They were part of the newly formed coalition of opposition forces in Britain christened the Kenya United Front for Democracy (KUFD), "whose members [were] amalgamated from several opposition parties" and who had come out in force "to peacefully demonstrate against the longest surviving African dictator who visited London from 16-18 November 1994 to hold meetings with the Confederation of British Industries (CBI)."[32] They used this medium to document not only human rights abuses of the Kenya government but also the various meetings that the opposition organized in various venues in London. These were high-profile venues, like the School of Oriental and African Studies, University of London, and Acton High School, situated in London. All the major opposition players made it to London to present their case to the international community. Among these included Koigi Wa Wamwere, James Orengo, Dennis Akumu, Paul Muite, and later, Raila Odinga.

This was the era of ethnic, ideological, and religious alliances. For the first time Muslims worked side by side with the Christian clergy in posing a real challenge to Moi. Among the notable sympathizers of the IPK was Reverend Dr. Timothy Njoya,[33] the iconoclastic Yale-educated theologian who was the most determined critic of the regime. Yet, in the final analysis, IPK politics was charismatic politics centered around the cult of Sheikh Balala. The local press in Kenya dubbed him the spiritual leader of the IPK, and by implication, of Kenya Muslims. Nothing could have been further from the truth. For Balala was neither a sheikh nor the spiritual leader of the Muslims in the country. Sheikh Balala was a high school dropout.

---

31 Published briefly in the early 1990s under the editorship of Bwantumu.

32 *Waswahili Voice,* vol. 1, June 28, 1997.

33 http://www.state.gov/j/drl/rls/hrrpt/1999/252.htm.

He had left the Allidina Visram High School, Mombasa, in the mid-1970s at Form Two, at the age of sixteen to seek his fortune in Saudi Arabia.[34] This was the peak of the oil boom, and many young Kenyan Muslims who could not make it through the highly competitive national high school entrance examination, the dreaded Kenya Certificate of Primary Education, headed to the wide world of the Saudi Arabian unskilled job market that was beckoning all and sundry. Balala found his niche there. When he left Kenya, it is inconceivable that he would have acquired enough Islamic education to enable him to give fatwas, as befits a spiritual leader. In the same vein, he could not have found his way into the rigid Saudi education system, with its medieval emphasis on rote learning, localized curriculum in the humanities, and the barring of even long-term residents from accessing university education in the kingdom.

What set Sheikh Balala apart from both the older brand of leaders and the emergent younger generation of leaders was the audacity with which he went about challenging Moi. He started off as a street preacher at Mwembe Tayari, strategically a shrewd point to select because it was the main rendezvous for all the Mombasa public transport, for all the directions across the island and beyond. The public was literally his captive audience. In fact, it has always been the place where fundamentalists of all stripes, Islamic and otherwise, carried on shouting matches in defense of their sectarian beliefs. It was here, under the prying eyes of Moi's agent provocateurs, that he began his journey from religious notoriety to national political attention.

He started not with Moi, in fact, but with Moi's proxies at the coast, Shariff Nassir Taib and Said Hemed, and accused them of selling out Muslims, using the most vulgar language that he could muster, and which would have shock value.[35]

He succeeded immensely in attracting large crowds which were there solely to savor Balala's obscene diatribes directed at his new nemeses; both Nassir and Hemed did not even know about him at first, but were eventually forced to pay attention to him. Once this strategy worked, he went directly for Moi's jugular. He indulged in all manner of name calling, from thief to faggot, a quite serious charge in a macho society like Kenya. Of course, the Kenyan laws then considered the person of the president

[34] Personal communication, Abdulaziz Ali Khamis, Balala's classmate at Allidina Visram High School, a chartered accountant, a one-time guest worker in Saudi Arabia, until recently the financial director, Wrigley, Kenya; Nairobi, April 10, 1992.

[35] This author, in the course of research, went to listen to these street preachers in 1992.

as almost sacrosanct and harsh treatment was reserved for those who libeled the president. As a consequence Balala was thrown in and out of prison innumerable times. The government prosecutors eventually decided to charge him with treason, whose punishment was no less than the death sentence.[36]

Whether the government was determined to carry through the sentence once he could be found guilty, which the judges then could easily have done, given the complicity of the judiciary in the perversion of justice because many of those on the bench were political appointees, remains a mystery to this day. He was defended pro bono by Taib Ali Taib, the young Muslim lawyer and political activist. Taib was later to defend individuals who were suspected of involvement in terrorist activities at the behest of the FBI.[37] He defended the suspects on the grounds that Kenya was a sovereign state and should not take orders from a foreign country, when the American government demanded their repatriation to face the American justice system. For Balala, needless to say, the charges were withdrawn and another strategy was employed, the more drastic one of stripping him of his citizenship. Whoever was charged with this winning strategy waited until Balala had traveled outside the country. When he reached Germany, it was conveyed to him that he was stripped of his citizenship because, it was alleged, he was born in Yemen, and therefore was a Yemeni, and not a Kenyan citizen.

At this time African governments were stripping their recalcitrant citizens of their nationality. Zambia had already declared Kenneth Kaunda, its founding father, a citizen of Malawi in order to bar him from contesting the presidency; so had Oscar Kambona in Tanzania.[38] Balala was of course born in Kenya. Balala's opposition supporters mobilized their following in order to challenge the constitutionality of the government's action.

In the words of the IPK London mouthpiece,

> Early in November, the Kenyan influential opposition leaders Hon. James Orengo and Professor Rashid Mzee—the First and Second Vice-Chairman of Ford Kenya, visited Germany to to discuss Balala's affair with the German members of parliament. According to our sources they were sympathetic and agreed to give this issue a serious consideration.[39]

---

[36] See note 27 above.

[37] http://www.guardian.co.uk/world/2002/nov/29/kenya.terrorismandtravel1.

[38] http://www.bbc.co.uk/news/world-africa-14423538.

[39] See "Balala's Citizenship Saga," *Waswahili Voice,* vol. 1, p. 10.

In a characteristic move, Balala opted to challenge the barely legitimate government by audaciously booking a ticket on Lufthansa back to Kenya whether the Moi government liked it or not. In a stage-managed, almost comical welcoming ceremony, all the major opposition leaders went to the airport to receive Balala à la head of state. In the lineup were Kenneth Matiba, Ngengi Muigai (FORD-Asili), Raila Odinga (National Development Party), and Paul Muite (SAFINA). Also in attendance were the media and the tourists arriving in the country. The opposition leaders received severe beatings from the police in their attempts to stop immigration officers from barring Sheikh Khalid Balala from disembarking from the aircraft.[40] Both local public and international opinion was against the mistreatment of Balala and the stripping of his citizenship. The government, wisely, relented and his citizenship was later restored.[41] But he was outside the country for sufficiently long for his mystique to wear out and for his popularity to wane. He failed to reinvent himself to meet the new and changed circumstances. Yet Balala was a major plank in the opposition's game plan to wear out Moi psychologically.

Sheikh Balala himself was actually marginal to the organizational aspects of the IPK. For one, the party strategists were better organized and focused and were under no illusion that the sailing was ever going to be smooth. They also realized they were likely to meet stiff opposition from among a section of the Muslim community itself because of vested interests that were inextricably tied to KANU. Some Muslims also felt that as Muslims they had collectively fared better under the Moi regime than they had done under Kenyatta, despite his Islamophobia. It was Moi, just as soon as he had emerged from the turbulent events of August 1982, who had appointed the first Muslim to a full ministerial position, however insignificant the portfolio itself may have been. Maalim Mohamed, the brother of General Mahmoud Mohammed who was instrumental in squashing the coup, was appointed the minister of culture in appreciation of his brother's role. He was the first Muslim ever in independent Kenya to hold a full ministerial position. Under Kenyatta, Muslims never got appointed beyond the positions of assistant ministers, and again these were only a handful.[42] To his credit, though, Kenyatta never adopted sectarian positions as the head of state. He cared very little for religion or displays of religious symbolism

[40] *Sunday Nation*, June 8, 1997.

[41] http://www.e-prism.org/images/Islam_in_Africa_Newsletter_-_No4_-_August06.pdf.

[42] See Bakari, "Muslims and the Politics of Change in Kenya."

and went out of his way to treat all citizens with equality, in keeping with his earlier promise, when he came to power, to maintain political harmony by practicing the politics of inclusion. He was, however, not averse to appointing a disproportionate number of Kikuyu ministers in all his cabinet appointments. He was obviously under pressure from his ethnic group to always tip the balance in their favor. This predominance of the Kikuyu not only in politics but also in economics and civil administration became the hallmark of the Kenyatta era. It was imprinted in the Kenyan political psyche that Kenyatta, and by extension the Kikuyu, did not respect proportionate representation in an ethnically diverse society.

The redeeming thing was that the Kenyan independence Constitution gave powers to the president to nominate twelve members of Parliament[43] in addition to the elected ones, and this gave Kenyatta the leeway to include minorities who might not, given the numbers game, ever have been elected on a popular vote. It was this important caveat that provided an opportunity for minority groups to be included in the legislative process to represent minority views. The problem here was that these nominated members of Parliament were actually used by the government to tip the balance in its favor wherever there might have been dissenting voices in the passing of some legislation; the nominated MPs often misread their nomination as requiring unquestioning loyalty to the government of the day, right or wrong.

These new political appointees gave Muslims a new lease on life and a sense of inclusion in a way they never felt during Kenyatta's administration. Moi's symbolic gesture, and the later closeness between him and General Mahmoud Mohammed, did a lot to attract ambitious Muslims to KANU, and more importantly, to quell Somali irredentism in the North Eastern Province. Muslims were gradually integrated within President Moi's gravy train, and a significant number of them made a fortune within the no-holds-barred corrupt system that was institutionalized. A number of Muslims have been as complicit as the others in raiding the national treasury. Currently it is believed that about 240 billion dollars in Kenyan

[43] *The Constitution of Kenya*. Published by the National Council for Law Reporting. See Section 97 (1) (c). Twelve members are nominated by parliamentary political parties according to their proportion of members of the national assembly (Constitution of Kenya, 2010). In the old constitution, this was first brought forward by the 1968 amendment to the constitution which gave the president authority to appoint twelve nominated members of Parliament.

currency is stashed in secret foreign accounts.[44] This monumental theft, the so-called Goldenberg Affair, still baffles Kenyans. Muslims also did partake of public land earmarked for development projects to benefit the general public. These ranged from school playgrounds, access roads, and hospital grounds to reserved forested areas.

Muslims and Civil Society

Meanwhile, the younger generation of better educated Muslims came of age and graduated from universities both locally and abroad. It was through these that the Muslims' niche in the new culture of non-governmental organizations (NGOs) was gradually assured. Increasingly, Muslims established their own community institutions and strengthened those that were already in place. These efforts cut across racial and sectarian divides. These were already in addition to foreign NGOs from the Middle East that purported to serve the interests of the Kenyan public. A number of these organizations were closed in the aftermath of the tragic bombing of the American embassies in Kenya and Tanzania on August 7, 1998. They were suspected of fronting terrorist activities. Especially noted was the Haramayn Foundation, with its solid Saudi Arabian connections,[45] and manned mostly by Somalis. Although these outfits served mostly in Muslim areas, and especially in areas bordering Somalia to cater to the needs of thousands of displaced refugees who were Muslims, they were invariably staffed by an assortment of Sudanese, Egyptians, Algerians, and Somalis. They made very little effort to involve Kenyan Muslims themselves in their activities. When they were singled out by the NGO Registration Board for closure, there were some outcries from the Muslim public, but these soon faded because they were seen as serving more the interests of the officials of the relevant NGOs than the interests of the Kenyan public.

The Decline of the Supreme Council of the Kenya Muslims and the Rise of the Muslim Consultative Council

The Supreme Council of Kenya Muslims (SUPKEM) was established as part of the grand strategy of the Kenyatta government to control various sections of Kenyan society in the early years of the Kenyatta

[44] *East African Standard,* May 20, 2004.

[45] http://www.un.org/sc/committees/1267/NSQE10504E.shtml.

administration,[46] from trade unions to religious organizations, in the name of centralization of decision making. The Supreme Council was established about the same time as the Central Organization of Trade Unions and the National Christian Council of Kenya. These were umbrella organizations that were created to provide direct channels of communication between the government and important and influential sectors of Kenyan society. All the organizations that served civil society were supposed to be affiliated to one or another of these umbrella bodies. And SUPKEM was intended to be the clearing ground for Muslim organizations that wanted to deal with the government. They could not deal directly with governmental bodies without clearing with it first. This privilege gave considerable powers to the organization. As a result, Muslim laypeople who could not exercise political power, but who were ambitious themselves, gravitated towards and jostled for power within SUPKEM. It was also a ready-made instrument for senior civil servants and ex-politicians who wanted to consolidate and secure their positions within the bureaucracy. As a result, it was perennially bogged down by infighting. By being part of SUPKEM, too, opportunities for travel, access to Middle Eastern funding, and other perks became readily available. While it started with little credibility from its inception, SUPKEM continued to battle against its negative image in the Muslim public eye.

By the 1990s the younger generation of better educated Muslims sought to establish alternative leadership by creating new institutions. One notable organization that was put in place was the Muslim Consultative Council (MCC).[47] In essence this was a coalition of Muslims from a variety of racial, ethnic, and sectarian backgrounds who wanted to take a more direct political role in the unfolding drama of the new opposition politics sparred by demands for multiparty democracy. These were young Muslim professionals drawn from the ranks of lawyers, accountants, doctors, university students, and managers of successful businesses. They felt that Muslims must take an active role in the new politics that were unfolding. A number of these individuals also belonged to the new opposition parties or even as part of the ruling KANU party, but wanted to present a distinctive Muslim voice. This became even more urgent when the idea of a new national constitution was mooted. They felt that Muslims must play an active role in the constitution-making process and get their interests protected. The

[46] See Mwakimako, "Politics, Ethnicity and the Jostling for Power."

[47] http://www.ogiek.org/sitemap/terrorism_bill.pdf.

first priority was the consolidation of the gains that already existed, ensuring that Muslim personal law, as embodied in the Kadhi Courts Act, was not tempered with. They wanted the Kadhis' courts to be enshrined in the Constitution. This was more urgent now than ever, given the rumblings of the Christian clergy and their concern with what was happening next door in the Sudan, and farther northwest in Nigeria, where the northern states were calling for, and in some instances actually implementing, the shari'a law,[48] much to the concern of non-Muslims there. In fact, one of the sticking points in the Sudanese political conflict in the south was the issue of the inappropriateness of applying the shari'a in a predominantly non-Muslim south. Nairobi was already the political base of the southern rebel movement under General John Garang, and pressure was being brought to bear on Muslims by the unprecedented demands by the Christian clergy in Kenya for the removal of the constitutional protection of the Kadhis' courts.

Muslims and the Politics of Constitution-Making

The Christian clergy's demand for the abolition of the Muslim courts was clearly externally driven, as a lot of contentious issues in the Christian church in Kenya were. For one, the Catholic Church was financed by the Vatican and all the decisions, just like the Catholic Church elsewhere, had to be cleared with Rome. On the other hand, Protestant and Anglican churches were also either stealthily manipulated or financed from the outside, and appeared to outsiders to be bidding to their masters from abroad.[49] They have been especially perceived by Muslims to be inspired from the outside and used by the West to fight its proxy wars with Muslims wherever they are since 9/11.

The Muslims themselves later did not help the situation when, carried away by overzealousness, they started seriously talking about having separate courts to adjudicate on Muslim commercial disputes. Apart from a lack of trained Muslim judges with competence to preside over such courts, there was the difficulty of establishing such courts in a state that was dedicated to secularism from its inception. The Kadhis' courts became one of the main bones of contention between the Christian church

[48] See Philip Ostien, ed., *Sharia Implementation in Northern Nigeria, 1999–2006: A Sourcebook*, vols. 1–5 (Ibadan, Nigeria: Spectrum Books, 2007).

[49] See J. M. Coetzee's review of Ali A. Mazrui's *The Africans* in *Stranger Shores: Essays 1986–1999* (Vintage Books, 2001), 245–46.

and the Muslims in Kenya. In fairness to the rest of the non-Muslim Kenyans, they could not care less if Muslims wanted to have Islamic law applied to themselves in matters of personal status. However, there were a lot of non-Muslims who defended the right of Muslims to continue with the status quo, in which the Kadhis' courts played an important role in the preservation of Muslim identity. Writing in the press, one such defender was Wycliffe Muga, who noted in a commentary that the clergy had no right to stop Muslims from enjoying their freedom of worship. He specifically singled out Rev. Mutava Musyimi, an influential official within the National Christian Council of Kenya and a suddenly vociferous critic of the Kadhis' courts. Muga noted that nearly two years, Rev. Mutava Musyimi had been the spokesman for the Ufangamano Initiative in its struggle to make significant input into the proposed new constitution. This may have led many to forget that he was not an expert on constitutional matters, that he was only a clergyman.

> By training, he probably is well equipped to teach people how to live morally upright lives. But, as has recently been revealed, he has little knowledge of how to handle the delicate minority rights issues when drafting a constitution.
>
> Those who support Rev. Musyimi's arguments that Kadhis' courts should be dealt with by routine parliamentary legislation fail to take into consideration two important points.
>
> The first is that—precisely because any such minorities will have limited powers to influence legislation—minority rights protection must necessarily be entrenched in that constitution.

Wycliffe Muga went on to add that the reverend needed to take note of certain points:

> Rev. Musyimi and his friends need to take note . . . that whatever may be their own views on the matter, to Kenya's Muslim minority, the Kadhis courts represent a fundamental religious freedom.
>
> It is one of the pillars of liberal democracy that minority rights (along with women's and other basic liberties) be studiously protected through constitutional provisions.
>
> Viewed from the perspective of democratic values and principles, any attempt to remove the kadhis' courts constitutional protection necessarily proposes gross injustice . . .

> The logical conclusion then is that any minority rights not protected by the constitution are likely to be trampled underfoot sooner or later on one pretext or another.
>
> The kadhis' courts, while benefiting Muslims only, do not in any way harm or inconvenience Christians, Hindus, or adherents of any other religions.
>
> Nobody who seeks to deny the Kadhis' courts any constitutional protection can claim to be acting in good faith or democratic principles.[50]

The clergy had been egged on to take the issue to the Kenyan High Court to challenge the inclusion of the Kadhis' courts in the new Draft Constitution. If the clergy did manage to have their way, this would have been one of the most explosive issues in Kenya and one that would have had dire consequences not only for Kenya, but would have repercussions throughout East Africa. Because both in the north and south, Kenya was bounded by Muslim majority countries, and with absolute anarchy in Somalia, the situation could spiral out of control. However, the country held a referendum on the new constitution and on August 4, 2010, 66 percent endorsed it, and the endorsement included the inclusion of the Kadhis' courts as legitimate courts to deal with Muslim personal law.[51] The potential religious strife was thus amicably resolved to the satisfaction of the majority of Kenyans.

Mohammed Omar Maluki, a member of the Supreme Council of Kenya Muslims representing the predominantly Kikuyu Central Province, writing in the *East Africa Standard* on May 22, 2004, among other things observed:

> It should be noted that the Kadhis' courts have been around since independence [*sic*]. They have never in any way affected Christians.
>
> The Kadhis' courts handle only marriage, divorce and inheritance matters. Never has a Muslim been stoned to death for adultery or his hand chopped off for stealing or killed for murdering or whipped for drinking alcohol.

---

[50] http://www.nationaudio.com/News/Daily Nation/03052003/ . . . /Comment03052003.htm. See also Kadhis' courts clause not negotiable, say Muslims: http://www.nationaudio.com/News/DailyNation/Todat/News/News1604200356.html; Ahmed Issack Hassan, "Kadhis Courts: Here Are the Facts," http://www.nationaudio.com/News/DAILYNATION/COM . . . /Comment240420031.htm.

[51] http://www.bbc.co.uk/news/world-africa-10856761.

> This clearly shows that the Kadhis' courts are only empowered to deal with domestic issues. I do not understand why the issue is causing rumpus among some Christians.
>
> Recently some Christians demonstrated in the Muslim dominated areas of Mombasa—a sign they were provoking Muslims. They later dispersed without achieving their goal.
>
> It should be noted that those who wanted change only wanted to remove Moi and KANU from power. They never wanted changes in the Constitution. This explains the petty, personalised differences over certain aspects of the Draft Constitution.[52]

The battle for controlling the Draft Constitution was increasingly turning out to be a very good barometer of the internal tensions with the NARC coalition, a coalition cobbled up by the merger of two within-opposition parties, the National Alliance Party of Kenya and the Liberal Democratic Party, with Raila Odinga clearly on the side of the Muslims and the Kikuyu faction on the side of the Kikuyu-led clergy. Those Muslims who are allied to the Kikuyu-led faction of NARC would increasingly find themselves in a dilemma.

The decade of the 1990s saw much increase in traffic between Kenya and the American Bible Belt, with evangelical Christians taking a keener interest in Kenya and virtually running the show for many "local" churches, since the latter are dependent on the Americans' wherewithal. Kenya is also the American evangelical staging post for their mission into southern Sudan. They seem to exert an undue influence on the Kenyan Pentecostal Church, among others, to oppose the rights that Muslims have enjoyed for over a century now, and just want them enshrined in the new constitution. There have also been complaints from Kenyan Muslims that there has been interference by Western diplomatic missions, most notably American and British, in this issue,[53] although these have been vigorously denied by both since this would be tantamount to interfering in the internal affairs of a sovereign state.

Although there might appear to be seemingly irreconcilable differences between Muslims' entrenched position and that of the Christians' mortal opposition on the issue of Kadhis' courts, these are no more than histrionic posturings calculated to impress the followers of the opposing

[52] http/:www.eastandard.net/commentaries/column/col03.htm.

[53] http//:www.article19.org/data/files/pdfs/publications/Kenya-censorship-in-kenya.pdf.

camps. The average Kenyan has economic hardships on his mind rather than these academic sparrings. On a lot of issues most Kenyans are at one, whether they are Muslims or Christians. For example, most Kenyans are capable of understanding the implications of international politics on the domestic situation. It was precisely because of this that there was hardly a backlash against Muslims when the bombing of the American Embassy in Nairobi took place. Although there was initial finger-pointing at Muslims, soon Kenyans came to their senses by realizing that among the victims of the bombing were several Muslims, and that Kenya was caught up in the intricacies of international politics. In contrast, the FBI operatives[54] went into Muslim areas with a swagger, harassed not only those suspected of involvement in the planning of the attacks, but also the family members of those alleged suspects. This was frowned upon by Kenyans of all backgrounds. No wonder that when the issue of attempts to pass an anti-terrorist bill through Parliament came, many Kenyans saw the American hand in the draft. In fact, many Kenyans saw that this was an attempt to roll back the hard-won gains of freedom of movement and assembly that Moi had severely curtailed. The majority of Kenyans were and are opposed to the passing of the bill that has an uncanny resemblance to the American Patriot Act which has aroused controversy even within America itself and which Kenyan Muslims perceive as especially targeted at them. The issue has been widely debated in the country. It was reported in the local press that most leaders were opposed to the provisions of the bill. The leading Kenyan daily, *The Nation,* carried this important news item:

> Law Society chairman Ahmednassir Abdullahi, speaking in a private capacity, described the law as unjust and draconian. He said some of its provisions contradicted the constitution.
>
> The others who spoke were lawyers Prof. Makau Mutua, chairman of the task force on Truth and Reconciliation, and Mr. Keriako Tobiko, a member of the Constitution of Kenya Review Commission.
>
> Prof. Mutua said: "If our Parliament passes this law, it will have taken away, with one blow, the basic rights of Kenyans and make irrelevant our quest for a new constitutional order. It is a piece of legislation that seeks to create a republic of fear, paranoia and a police state."
>
> He and Mr. Abdullahi said it was being imposed by American and British governments.

[54] http://www.guardian.co.uk/world/2002/nov/29/kenya.terrorismandtravel1.

> Said Dr. Abdullahi: "It is an unconstitutional and outrageous bill that abrogates all rights of human beings. It kills due process and is not a Bill for a civilized country." Speaking to the Sunday Nation, Mr. Abdullahi said if the Bill is passed by Parliament in its current state it would kill "due process." He argued that the Bill empowered other countries to "abuse" the sovereignty of the country by allowing them to conduct "haphazard arrests any time and in any place."[55]

In any case, the shari'a has been operative since the inception of the colony in 1895, and its recognition goes back to the independent state in 1963. In reality, it was after the constitutional guarantee for restoration of the Kadhis'[56] courts as part of the Kenyan judicial system at the Lancaster House Conference, 1963, that the sultan of Zanzibar's jurisdiction over the Kenyan Coastal strip was passed on to the new independent state.

It was the aim of the MCC to prepare a strategy that would enable Muslims not only to consolidate past gains but look forward to a future that was more democratic and open for Kenya as a whole, which had never happened since the early years of independence. They succeeded in holding a number of meetings to work out modalities of the Muslim position within the unfolding constitutional debates and the voting strategies in the coming elections. Among the MCC's prominent members were Murtaza Jaffer, a prominent Shia University of Dar es Salaam-educated political activist, human rights lawyer, and the secretary of the National NGO Council; Farouk Adam, a scion of one of the most prominent Asian business families; Abdulrahman Wandati, the secretary and founder member of the unregistered IPK; and Swaleh Kanyeki, a prominent Nairobi lawyer, among many others.[57] Through effective strategizing and networking with non-Muslim organizations both religious and secular, the MCC was able to contribute significantly in assembling an effective team of individuals that were to be nominated to the National Constitutional Review Commission (CRC), which was mandated to prepare a new national constitution

---

[55] http//:www.nationaudio.com/News/dailyNation/29062003/News/News2906200347.html.

[56] For a fuller treatment of the issue of Kadhis' courts, see Hassan Mwakimako, "The Evolution of Chief Kadhiship in Kenya: 1895–1963" (Ph.D. thesis, University of Cape Town, 2003).

[57] See Hashim A. Abdulkadir, "Reforming and Retreating: British Policies on Transforming the Administration of Islamic Law and Its Institutions in the Busa'idi Sultanate, 1890–1963" (Ph.D. thesis, University of Western Cape, 2010).

after wide consultations throughout the country. In the final Muslim lineup Muslims were able to have a strong team that included women representatives like Mrs. Abida Ali and others who reflected Islam's diversity in Kenya. It is significant too that the first vice-chairman of the CRC, a Muslim, Professor A. I. Salim, was nominated for this position.

It is also important to record that some individuals played an important role in bringing on board non-Muslim opinion in sympathizing with constitutional issues that affected Muslims. One such person was Professor Ali A. Mazrui, the distinguished Kenyan-American political scientist resident in the United States, and later the chancellor of Jomo Kenyatta University of Agriculture and Technology. Through public lectures and publications he put forth Muslim perspectives on a number of national issues. It also helped that he had personal rapport with a number of key figures in the Review Commission, most notably the commission chairman, Professor Yash Pal Ghai. The latter invited Ali Mazrui to give public lectures under his commission's auspices.[58] It is noteworthy that Yash Pal Ghai is a Kenyan Hindu and a professor of constitutional law at the University of Hong Kong.

New Leadership for a New Era: The Rise of the Muslim Technocrat as Spokesman

The expansion of educational opportunities in the decades of the 1980s and 1990s created a large pool of educated Kenyans of all ethnic and religious backgrounds. Although for a considerable time Muslims lagged behind other religious groups in their acquisition of secular education, that was not exactly the case with religious education per se. Beginning in the mid-1970s, as indicated earlier, relatively large numbers of Muslims had headed to the Middle Eastern universities to pursue Islamic studies in the major universities there. The Kenyan Somalis were the majority of those who went to the Islamic University in Medina, followed by coastal Muslims of primarily the Digo and Bajuni ethnic groups. Most of these were graduates of local madrasas whose syllabi were geared towards the admission demands of those institutions. Although they were not fully prepared for either Saudi or Egyptian university entry examinations, their admission was made more flexible by taking into account that the students did not come from an Arabic-speaking country and provision was made for

[58] Personal communication, Ali Mazrui, Istanbul, May 2011.

them to acquire better linguistic skills to prepare them for university studies. It must be added that the generous scholarships, in conformity with the general Saudi view, were not extended to women. And all the prospective students were admitted to the Islamic University in Medina only, and with only a few going to other Saudi universities. It was the Saudi version of the Soviet Union's Lumumba International University which only admitted students from the Third World.[59]

This arrangement was reminiscent of the Kenyan students who were airlifted to Russia after Oginga Odinga managed to secure university admissions into Russian universities, where they were required to undergo a six-month intensive course in the Russian language.[60]

The graduates of theological and Islamic studies were often those who had terminated their secular education in the early stages and opted to concentrate on their chosen field of specialization. The downside to this choice was that many of these graduates from Islamic universities became alienated from the mainstream Kenyan society on account of their educational backgrounds and virtually lived insulated from the larger secular society. This tended to color their view of the wider world and could hardly provide viable leadership to their Muslim brethren within the wider Kenyan contexts. Their spiritual leadership was mostly confined to providing religious guidance in mosques or to their charges in the Saudi-linked madrasas where many of them taught. The lucky few found their way into clerical jobs in Arab embassies where Arabic linguistic skills were in demand. In the mid-1970s a number of them were employed as translators from Arabic to English, although their skills in English were rather inadequate. They however were able to make a decent living, sometimes even better than graduates from the local universities.

It was in fact the graduates from the Kenyan universities and those from abroad who provided a better leadership for the Kenyan Muslims because they understood their environment and the wider world more than did their theologically trained co-religionists. These were the ones who, though less well paid, left the most impact in the Muslims' dealings with the other Kenyans. It is they who were well integrated within Kenyan society and who held jobs in the national bureaucracy, business, and politics. A number of them were actually well-known national figures, whose fame

---

[59] See Bakari, "The New Ulama in Kenya."

[60] See Oginga Odinga, *Not Yet Uhuru: An Autobiography,* African Writers Series (Heinemann, 1968).

rested more on their own individual merit, skills, and education than on their religious background. Indeed, these are as secularized as the majority of the Kenyans. They are often at ease in their dealings with their compatriots regardless of their religious orientation. Since they often went to the same universities, the same faculties, and sometimes even the same departments with fellow non-Muslim Kenyans, they have forged lasting friendships and relations with people outside their religious orbit, whether from medical school, art school, or law school. These contacts served them in good stead in their professional lives in the future. Included in this group are the hundreds of Muslim women who have similarly benefited from secular education in institutions of higher learning both in Kenya and abroad.

Within this group, interestingly, must be included the recently retired chief kadhi of Kenya, Sheikh Hammad Muhammad Kassim Mazrui, who had taken over the kadhiship from Sheikh Nassor Nahdi. Sheikh Hammad is a scion of the well-known Mazrui family of Mombasa, whose father was himself the chief kadhi of Kenya for many years in the late 1950s to 1968, when he retired. He is also a brother to Professor Alamin Mazrui, the well-known Kenyan playwright, a former political detainee, a human rights campaigner, and a noted scholar currently teaching at Rutgers University, New Jersey. Hammad studied physics at the University of Mosul, Iraq, and during the eight-year Iraq-Iran war relocated to the University of Riyadh. He later went to the University of Ibadan, Nigeria, to pursue a master's degree in Islamic studies. He taught for a while at the Sheikh Khalif Bin Zayd School, Mombasa, the leading Muslim institution in Kenya and one of the top ten private schools in the country. His tenure as the chief kadhi proved less contentious than had the previous kadhiships. Having just retired, Sheikh Hammad has been succeeded by Sayyid Ahmad Muhdhar Hussein, a graduate of the University of Kuwait.

Other Muslims have held important positions in the civil service and many more are in the private sector holding important positions. Muslims have from time to time within this decade been elected to influential and prestigious chairmanships of such bodies as the brahmin Law Society of Kenya, the International Commission of Jurists (Kenya Chapter), and the Kenya Medical Association. A number of Muslims have held the position of High Court judges and Industrial Court judges, among others. Kenya has also had its first Muslim commissioner of police in the recent past. Within the Kenyan context appointments to high office are loaded with symbolism, since they signal the inclusion or exclusion of particular groups. For example, once the Somalis ceased their irredentism, Somali individuals were appointed to responsible positions in droves, sometimes far out of proportion to their numerical strength. And so, while the Somalis themselves rejoiced at these turns of fortune, Muslims interpreted these gestures as acts of recognition of Muslims as equal citizens, accorded a place at the table. When Moi left office there were almost eleven ambassadors and high commissioners representing Kenya abroad. These have included the strategic posting in Washington, with Dr. Yusuf Abdulrahman Nzibo as the ambassador there. A historian of Latin America, he trained in the universities of Nairobi and Glasgow, before pursuing an M.B.A. at the London Business School. He also served as the commissioner general of the Kenya Revenue Authority. He was until recently Kenya's ambassador in Riyadh. He was married to Dr. Sally Kosgei, a Kipsigis, and the most powerful woman in the Moi government, as head of the civil service. She was a classmate of Condoleezza Rice at Stanford University.[61] She has since gone into politics and is the current minister of agriculture in the Mwai Kibaki coalition government.[62]

Young Muslims and Higher Education

A group of professional Muslims are currently looking at the possibility of establishing a Muslim university at the coast that will enroll students from all backgrounds and that will teach subjects that are relevant to Kenya's present needs, with a faculty of Islamic studies dedicated to the production of locally trained ulama who are in tune with the mood of the country, and who will be expected to understand its past historical struggles and aspirations for the future. It had been seen that the foreign-trained ulama have imbibed ideologies that were not consonant with the demands of a multi-religious and secular society. The feasibility study has been done by one of the most noted land economists in Kenya, Professor Saad Yahya, who until recently headed the Department of Land Economics at the University of Nairobi. He has over the years done projects for Habitat, the United Nations body overseeing the provision of decent housing internationally. The university project is likely to benefit from Islamic Development Bank funding. The latter organization has for the past twenty years sponsored Kenyan Muslim students for university education in engineering, medicine, and agriculture in leading Turkish state universities, many

[61] Personal communication, Nairobi, 1997.

[62] http//:www.statehousekenys.go.ke/index.htm.

of whom have returned to serve the nation in productive and meaningful ways.[63]

On the other hand, the same cannot be said of the graduates of religious institutions, who tend to see the world in black and white, and whose education ill equips them for life in a multi-religious and secular society. It puts them in a corner, with a captive audience of ill-educated people whose sole source of information and education is the Friday sermon, a format that is hardly enough to take in serious issues. The Friday sermons in the Wahhabi-led mosques, whose imams are alumni of Medina Islamic University, are very outspoken on issues like those of Iraq and Palestine, regardless of whether they have a good grasp of the historical forces that shaped these geopolitical situations. Their ideological positions are lent credibility by what the ordinary Kenyan Muslim sees on cable TV and, for the more information technology-savvy, through the Internet. Kenyan Muslims have been tuning in to Middle Eastern media for well over fifteen years now. And of course Al Jazeera has a significant audience among East African Muslims. The level of competence in Arabic has gone up for a variety of reasons, not the least being the impact of madrasa education, which now concentrates more on the acquisition of Arabic as a language of conversation and Islamic education. Arabic has been taught as a university subject at the University of Nairobi's Department of Linguistics and African Languages for almost two decades now to scores of students, with the majority of students being non-Muslims, who have found jobs in the diplomatic service, the media, and multinational corporations in the Middle East.

The first Kenyan with a Ph.D. in Arabic studies, Dr. Angaluki Muaka, graduated from UCLA, where he still remains, after having earned his undergraduate degree at the University of Nairobi. John Ogola, one of the earliest students of Arabic studies from Nairobi who graduated with a first class degree, opted to join the diplomatic service after serving initially as a personal assistant to the late Dr. Robert Ouko. He has served in Kenyan missions in Tokyo and Tehran. Others have gone to Pakistan to pursue postgraduate studies there. Arabic is no longer a novelty, but is just one of the languages that Kenyans find can be useful and learn purely for pragmatic and strategic reasons, just as they have done with German, French, and Italian.[64]

---

[63] See Mohamed Bakari, "Turkish-African Sociocultural Relations," in *Rising Africa and Turkey: Ist International Turkish-African Congress (23 November, 2005),* ed. Ahmet Kavas and Hasan Öztürk (Istanbul: TASAM Yayinlar, 2006).

[64] For Muslim politics in Kenya, see Mohamed Bakari, "Muslims and the Politics of Change in Kenya, 1963–1992," in *Islam in Kenya: Proceedings of the National Seminar on Contem-*

Conclusion

It is clear that relative to Muslims in the surrounding countries, Kenyan Muslims have been very well integrated within the Kenyan political system, and both Christians and Muslims have worked out a modus vivendi in their dealings with each other. Despite appearances of conflict, the two groups actually get along pretty well, and it is the tolerance of the majority and the adaptability of the minority that has enabled Kenya to be an island of tranquillity amidst utter chaos outside its borders. This relatively calm situation may be disturbed by undue interferences from outside in shaping the course of events in the country. And the issue of Muslim personal law could have had adverse effect on all the previous gains that the governments have modestly achieved despite their imperfections. This could also have had negative impact on the region's governments' attempts to fight against international terrorism. There might be future attempts to tamper with the law to dilute Muslim personal rights gains in the Constitution as it currently exists. If this does happen, it may shake the current facade of calmness.

One interesting development is that for the first time, the powerful office of chief justice of Kenya is currently held by Dr. Willy Mutanga, a Muslim convert from Catholicism.[65] During his vetting, the Catholic clergy tried to make into a national issue the fact that Mutunga is a Muslim. But the rest of the country did not go along with them. It is worth noting that in the case of the death of the president or his resignation, according to the Kenya Constitution, the chief justice acts as the interim president for the three months before the election of the next president. This is yet another indicator of the degree of integration that Muslims have attained since independence in 1963.

Bibliography

Ahmed, Leila. *A Quiet Revolution: The Veil's Resurgence from the Middle East to America.* New Haven, Conn.: Yale University Press, 2011.

Bakari, Mohamed. "Muslims and the Politics of Change in Kenya." In *Islam in Kenya: Proceedings of the National Seminar on Contemporary Islam in Kenya,* ed. Mohamed Bakari and Saad Yahya. Nairobi: Mewa, 1995.

---

porary Islam in Kenya, ed. Mohamed Bakari and Saad Yahya (Nairobi: Mewa, 1995). See also Oded, *Islam and Politics in Kenya.*

[65] See *Daily Nation,* August 23, 2012.

———. "The New Ulama in Kenya." In *Islam in Kenya: National Seminar on Islam in Contemporary Kenya*, ed. Mohamed Bakari and Saad Yahya. Nairobi: Mewa, 1995.

———. *The Secularization of Kenya Muslims: From Marginalization to Reinvention*. Unpublished Manuscript.

Bayart, Jean-François. *The State in Africa*. 2nd edition. Polity, 2009.

Gaffney, Patrick. *The Prophet's Pulpit: Islamic Preaching in Contemporary Egypt (Comparative Studies on Muslim Societies)*. Columbia University Press, 2009.

Hansen, Holger Bernt, and Michael Twaddle, eds. *Religion and Politics in East Africa: The Period Since Independence.* London: James Currey, 1995.

Hefner, Robert W., and Muhammad Qassim Zaman. *Schooling Islam: The Culture and Politics of Muslim Education*. Princeton, N.J.: Princeton University Press, 2007.

Hirji, Zulfikar, ed. *Diversity and Pluralism in Islam: Historical and Contemporary Discourse Among Muslims*. I. B. Tauris, 2010.

Kress, Kai. *Philosophising in Mombasa*. Edinburgh University Press, 2007.

Loimeier, Roman. *Between Social Skills and Marketable Skills: The Politics of Islamic Education in 20th-Century Zanzibar*. Leiden: Brill, 2009.

Loimeier, Roman, and Rüdiger Seesemann. *The Global Worlds of the Swahili: Interfaces of Islam, Identity and Space in 19th and 20th Century East Africa.* Berlin: LIT Verlag, 2006.

Mahmood, Saba. *Politics of Piety: Islamic Revival and the Feminist Subject.* Princeton, N.J.: Princeton University Press, 2005.

Mwakimako, Hassan. "The Ulama and the Colonial State in the Protectorate of Kenya: Politics, Ethnicity, and the Jostling for Power: The Evolution of the Institutions of Muslim Leadership and Kadhiship in Colonial Kenya, 1895 to 1965." Ph.D. thesis, University of Cape Town, 2003.

Ndzovu, Hassan J. *Religion and Politics: The Politicisation of Islam in Kenya.* Forthcoming. Evanston, Ill.: Northwestern University Press.

Oded, Arye. *Islam and Politics in Kenya.* Lynne Reinner, 2000.

Roy, Olivier. *Globalized Islam: The Search for the New Ummah.* CERI Series in Comparative Politics and International Studies. Columbia University Press, 2006.

Salim, Ahmed Idha. The *Swahili-Speaking Communities of Kenya's Coast, 1895–1965*. Nairobi: East African Publishing House, 1972.

Zaman, Muhammad Qassim. *The Ulama in Contemporary Islam: Custodians of Change.* Princeton, N.J.: Princeton University Press, 2002.

ARTICLES

Re-Creating Touba: Pilgrimage Videos in the American Muridiyya

Jeremy Dell, UNIVERSITY OF PENNSYLVANIA

DOI: 10.5192/21540993040149

ABSTRACT

This article examines the relationship between new media objects and novel religious practices through a consideration of pilgrimage videos available in American Murid communities. Building upon earlier studies of Murid visual culture, it suggests a preliminary typology of videos centered on the Grand Magal in Touba and the Magal of Two Rakkas in Saint-Louis. I argue that such videos, while not a substitute for pilgrimage itself, approximate the pilgrimage experience via their internal organization and formal characteristics. In addition to mediating religious practices within dispersed Murid communities, pilgrimage videos are also acts of historicization, rewriting narratives of Murid expansion within Senegal and without.

If his business card is any indication, Khadim Ndiaye's boutique Touba Khassida on the 200 block of West 116th Street in New York City is a one-stop retail experience for disciples of the Muridiyya, one of West Africa's best known (and most studied) Sufi orders. In a rough semicircle on the card, images of prayer beads flank a prayer mat, a bound volume with gold leaf patterning on the cover, a CD-ROM of "Le Saint Coran," and a box of Temple of Heaven China Green Tea, Special Gunpowder edition (figure 1). Turn the card over and find an advertisement for Daouda Touba, an electronics store selling international calling cards, cell phone batteries, and Apple iPhones. Together, the two sides of the card offer potential customers

Islamic Africa, VOL. 4, NO. 1, 2013. ISSN 2154-0993. www.islamicafricajournal.org

Figure 1
Images of communication devices adorn a two-sided business card for a Murid-owned shop in New York.

many of the tools that enable Murid disciples to maintain proper religious practice, sociability, and connections with far-flung friends and relatives. The juxtaposition of a prayer mat and a cell phone—two devices that enable distinctive yet, in the context of a dispersed religious community like the Muridiyya, complementary modes of communication—underscores the affinities between technological resources, group formation, and acceptable religious practice.

Touba Khassida and Daouda Touba are in fact two sides of the same shop. Upon entering, customers find the space neatly divided in half. To the left, a glass case displaying copies of the Qur'an, introductory guides to Islam, and informational pamphlets on the life of Amadu Bamba. Towards the back, but still on the left, oranges, yellows, and blues form a colorful patchwork on the wall. These would be photocopies of Bamba's poetry, along with the works of other major Murid poets, composed in Arabic as well as Wolofal, the graphic method by which Wolof is transcribed via Arabic script.[1] Turning to the right, customers are greeted with items of a different order. Here, in the Daouda Touba section of the shop, one finds cell phones, MP3 players, and digital cameras. Though less prominently displayed, Nigerian video films are also visible behind the counter. At a neutral midpoint between the wall of devotional poetry and the wall of electronic equipment sits the shared cash register and, behind it, a framed photo of Serigne Saliou Mbacké (d. 2007), the last son of Amadu Bamba and the fifth caliph of the Muridiyya. Positioned thus, the caliph's image looks out over the space of the shop, observing all transactions taking place within its walls.

To end a description of Touba Khassida/Daouda Touba here, however, would mean overlooking the shop's most extensive display of goods. Near the entrance, across from the Nigerian video films (and thus in the realm of Touba Khassida), one finds a much larger collection of DVDs devoted solely to religious matters. The stacked discs form a solid gray mass on the wall, a contrast from the riot of color that makes up the collection of printed poetry. Their contents are diverse: taped recordings of *dhikr*—remembrances of God through prayer, song and movement—*xutba*s treating a range of topics, documentaries about the life of Amadu Bamba, histories of Touba, histories of Islam in Senegal, and other subjects. On the counter before the wall of discs sit a television and a DVD player, where anyone authorized to make a sale can test the quality of the merchandise, demonstrating to prospective customers the reliability of Touba Khassida's DVDs. A video may in fact already be playing, with the images and sounds of chanting *taalibe*s and Murid shaykhs emanating throughout the shop as customers talk, take tea, chat on their cell phones, and sometimes even make purchases. Customers and neighbors may come and go, and the video may not be the object of anyone's focused attention, but it is no less

[1] For a more extensive treatment of the use of Wolofal in religious instruction, see Fallou Ngom, "Ahmadu Bamba's Pedagogy and the Development of 'Ajamī Literature," *African Studies Review* 52, no. 1 (2009): 99–124.

present for it. Whether or not one has come to Touba Khassida for Murid videos, one has entered a space whose visual and acoustic architecture is marked by their presence.[2]

Situating Video

Scenes like the one sketched above should be familiar to anyone who has ever patronized Murid-owned shops and households, whether in Senegal or elsewhere. These are spaces imbued with the images and sounds of Murid practice, a set of audiovisual cues that index the production of Murid space. But the apparently seamless incorporation of audiovisual material obscures just how recently televisions and DVD players became regular features of Murid sociability. Much of this of course owes to the price and portability of DVD technology itself. Like its predecessor the videocassette, the DVD has drastically altered the circulation of videos on the African continent and in the wider diaspora. The most conspicuous example of this trend has undoubtedly been the growth of the Nigerian video film industry, or "Nollywood," which perhaps trails only its obvious alter-referents (Bollywood, Hollywood) in terms of reach and productivity.[3] Though scaled to a smaller audience than its Nollywood counterpart, Murid video has also proliferated in recent years, offering a window onto changing media practices in the African diaspora, and their place in transnational religious communities.[4]

---

[2] Like many Murid texts, this paper employs a hybrid orthography. Frequently encountered terms such as "Touba" and "magal" appear in their common, French-Latinized form, even though official Senegalese Wolof orthography stipulates "Tuubaa" and "màggal" respectively. "Murid" has been preferred to the French rendering "Mouride" due to its ubiquity in English-language texts, while the plural forms of nouns are indicated with a terminal "s" despite the existence of postnominal determiners in Wolof (i.e., *taalibe bi* for "the student/disciple," *taalibe yi* for "the students/disciples"). The guiding principle has been to provide readers with the most useful terms for their own Internet searches. Entering the name "Mbacké" in a search engine, for example, will yield far more results than the "correct" spelling, "Mbàkke."

[3] For a helpful overview, with particular attention to regional styles, see chap. 6, "Extravagant Aesthetics: Instability and the Excessive World of Nigerian Film," in Brian Larkin, *Signal and Noise: Media, Infrastructure, and Urban Culture in Nigeria* (Durham, N.C.: Duke University Press, 2008). See as well the articles collected in Jonathan Haynes, ed., *Nigerian Video Films* (Athens: Ohio University Press, 2000).

[4] And like Nigerian video films, many Murid videos could be said to be "pirated" in the sense that unauthorized copies are regularly produced and sold; they have never been the

Videos are but one example of a host of media that have garnered attention from scholars of religion in recent years. Expanding the purview of the academic study of religion beyond conventional text-driven studies, this scholarship examines radio, television, cassettes, and other audiovisual materials in order to explore the sensuous realm of phenomena deemed "religious." The scholarly communities that have led this shift in focus have been sizable enough to produce a number of edited volumes organized around the paired terms "religion" and "media," and even a collection of "Key Words" in the tradition of Raymond Williams.[5] In addition to encouraging scholars of religion to widen the range of materials that form the empirical base of their research, these studies have also advocated reading the concept of media back onto more conventional objects of study (texts, rituals, etc.). From this perspective, the electronic communication devices that we usually associate with the term "media" become part of a longer history that includes, in the words of one scholar of religious media, "substances such as incense or herbs, sacrificial animals, icons, sacred books, holy stones and rivers, and, finally, the human body."[6]

Applied to the Murid case, this line of reasoning would inevitably lead to the figure of the shaykh. In an ideal-typical model of Murid religious practice, the figure of the shaykh is central, one that acts as a medium insofar as he mediates his disciples' relationship with the divine, deriving the authority to do so from his own devotion to Amadu Bamba, the Muridiyya's founder. This is one way in which religious practice is "mediated," whereas watching footage of a shaykh on a DVD adds yet another level of mediation to this relationship. But they are both equally forms of media, or so the argument goes, and as such act less as empty, neutral vessels waiting to be filled with a predetermined doctrine than as preconditions for the manifestation of religion itself. "Religion" is thereby reconceptualized as a

target of massive seizures of the kind that took place in November 2010, when more than 10,000 DVDs were confiscated from nine stores in Flatbush, Brooklyn. See Kareem Fahim, "Pirated Films from Nigeria Are Seized in Brooklyn," *New York Times*, November 4, 2010.

[5] See Hent de Vries and Samuel Weber, eds., *Religion and Media* (Palo Alto, Calif.: Stanford University Press, 2001); Birgit Meyer and Annelies Moors, eds., *Religion, Media, and the Public Sphere* (Bloomington: Indiana University Press, 2006); David Morgan, ed., *Key Words in Religion, Media and Culture* (New York: Routledge, 2008); Birgit Meyer, ed., *Aesthetic Formations: Media, Religion, and the Senses* (New York: Palgrave Macmillan, 2009).

[6] Birgit Meyer, "Introduction: From Imagined Communities to Aesthetic Formations: Religious Mediations, Sensational Forms, and Styles of Binding," in *Aesthetic Formations: Media, Religion, and the Senses* (New York: Palgrave Macmillan, 2009), 11.

process and practice of mediation, and its history becomes an inquiry into how newly utilized media challenge, replace, incorporate, or complement already established practices.[7]

It will probably come as little surprise that collapsing different instances of mediation into a single, all-encompassing category has not gained universal assent. Such an argument, according to Charles Hirschkind, is rooted in a specifically Protestant opposition of interior states and external practice in which practices "appear as mediatic vehicles enabling the manifestation of (internal) religiosity" rather than as constitutive elements of a religious tradition.[8] "The printed Quran does not mediate the traditions of Islam," Hirschkind continues; "the variety of ways the Quran is touched, held, cared for, read, recited, cherished, as well as printed and circulated are simply part of what is entailed in living as a Muslim."[9] Here, the disagreement seems to turn on whether calling a particular practice "mediated" is to necessarily treat it as external to a religious tradition (separate from that which is "simply . . . entailed in living as a Muslim"), or whether all such practices are "mediated" by definition. Perhaps such anxieties speak to the very ambivalences intrinsic to any particular medium. "Inseparable from the movement of social life and yet removed from it," writes William Mazzaerella, "a medium is thus at once obvious and strange, indispensable and uncanny, intimate and distant."[10]

Though scholars may differ on the nature of mediation and its relation to (or convergence with) religion, recognizing the importance of electronic media to contemporary religious movements is fairly uncontroversial.[11] Of

---

[7] In his introduction to *Key Words*, David Morgan credits Jesús Martín-Barbero with originating the idea of mediation, while Birgit Meyer associates the religion-as-mediation argument with the Dutch philosopher Hent de Vries. See Martín-Barbero, *Communication, Culture, and Hegemony: From the Media to Mediations*, trans. Elizabeth Fox and Robert A. White (London: Sage, 1993); Hent de Vries, "In Media Res: Global Religion, Public Spheres, and the Task of Contemporary Comparative Religious Studies," in de Vries and Weber, eds., *Religion and Media.* For a discussion of mediation as the cornerstone of social processes in general (and not only those deemed "religious"), see William Mazzarella, "Culture, Globalization, Mediation," *Annual Review of Anthropology* 33 (2004): 345–67.

[8] Charles Hirschkind, "Media, Mediation, Religion," *Social Anthropology/Anthropologie Sociale* 19 (2011): 93.

[9] In similar fashion, "the soccer ball does not mediate the game; it is a constitutive and necessary element within it." See Hirschkind, "Media, Mediation, Religion," 93.

[10] Mazzarella, "Culture, Globalization, Mediation," 346.

[11] In addition to the works already cited, see Charles Hirschkind, *The Ethical Soundscape: Cassette Sermons and Islamic Counterpublics* (New York: Columbia University Press,

course, the sheer quantity of such media artifacts can be bewildering. Students of the Muridiyya, however, can turn to two of the most prominent scholars of Murid visual practice, Allen F. and Mary Nooter Roberts. Their 2003 *A Saint in the City* offers a detailed and nuanced analysis of murals, posters, reverse-glass paintings, and other forms of Murid artistic expression. Drawing upon David Morgan's notion of "visual piety," defined here as "the set of practices, attitudes, and ideas invested in images that structure the experience of the sacred,"[12] the Robertses argue that images of Amadu Bamba actually exert themselves. They have the power to protect, to heal, to bless. Of course, such ideas are not the Robertses' invention, but are found in the interviews with Murid artists that the Robertses cite throughout their work. Combining formalistic/iconographic descriptions and analyses of images' social efficacy, such scholarship situates itself at the nexus of anthropology and art history.

A Saint in the City advocates placing the circulation of images at the center of an analysis of religious networks and the consolidation of group identity. Recent scholarship in religious studies tends to resonate with this approach, to the point of advocating it as an acceptable trans-cultural generalization. Building on the canonical work of Benedict Anderson, Birgit Meyer has held that modern imaginations of community must "become tangible outside the realm of the mind, by creating a social environment that materializes through the structuring of space, architecture, ritual performance, and by inducing bodily sensations."[13] Meyer revises Anderson's notion of imagined community as an "aesthetic formation." "*Aisthesis*," Meyer insists elsewhere, is not to be understood here as dealing with the nature of beauty, but instead refers "to our total sensorial experience of the world and our sensuous knowledge of it."[14] Such a reformulation priori-

2006); Brian Larkin, "Ahmed Deedat and the Form of Islamic Evangelism," *Social Text* 26, no. 3 (2008): 101–21; Dorothea E. Schulz, *Muslims and New Media in West Africa: Pathways to God* (Bloomington: Indiana University Press, 2012).

[12] David Morgan, *Visual Piety: A History and Theory of Popular Religious Images* (Berkeley: University of California Press, 1998), 2–3. Cited in Allen F. Roberts and Mary Nooter Robers, *A Saint in the City: Sufi Arts of Urban Senegal* (Los Angeles: University of California Fowler Museum of Cultural History, 2003), 73.

[13] Meyer, "Introduction," in Meyer, ed., *Aesthetic Formations*, 5.

[14] Brigit Meyer and Jojada Verrips, "Aesthetics," in Morgan, ed., *Key Words in Religion, Media and Culture*, 21 (emphasis in the original). Here Meyer and Verrips were building on Susan Buck-Morss's seminal reworking of Benjamin. See Susan Buck-Morss, "Aesthetics and Anaesthethics: Walter Benjamin's Artwork Essay Reconsidered," *October* 62 (1992): 3–41.

tizes "the role of shared images in forging links between individuals, organizing them into communities . . . images [that] mobilize and thrive upon shared sentiments, inducing modes, and moods, of feeling together."[15] Like the still images analyzed by the Robertses, Murid videos also provide external representations that visualize the very process by which communities are organized, a process centered on the re-creation of Touba in DVD format as a means of occasioning moments of "feeling together."

What follows is a preliminary typology of these videos, fairly loose in its method of categorization and far from exhaustive. With these qualifications in mind, it bears emphasizing the preliminary quality of these "findings." Many DVDs are devoted to pilgrimages, the most important being the annual pilgrimage to the holy city of Touba in the Diourbel region of central Senegal, roughly 200 kilometers from the capital of Dakar. Secondary pilgrimages include one to Saint-Louis and another to Porokhane, the village in east-central Senegal where Amadu Bamba's mother, Soxna Jaara Buso, is buried. A major Murid figure in her own right, her tomb is an especially popular pilgrimage destination for female Murids, and while videos of the pilgrimage to Porkohane will not be treated at length in this article, they do illustrate how media are intertwined with the potentially unstable gendered aspects of religious practice.[16]

Finally, it bears mentioning that pilgrimage videos not only circulate as DVDs, but are also increasingly available online, allowing Murid disciples to take part in "devotional surfing," to use a term coined by the Italian anthropologist Paolo Apolito. Referring to Catholic visionaries in the United States, Apolito suggests that "a new type of pilgrimage has become possible on the Web . . . allowing one to reach the venerated sacred image instantly; it could even make the physical trip unnecessary."[17] While perhaps not diminishing a disciple's desire to return to Touba, pilgrimage DVDs nevertheless allow for a measure of distant participation. The decentralized circulation of Murid video, whether via the Internet or physical DVDs, could just as well lead to more distracted forms of viewing. Even so, the ubiquity of Murid videos seems to suggest a certain utility with respect to contemporary Murid practice and the imbrication of the audiovisual with mundane experiences of the sacred.

[15] Meyer, "Introduction," in Meyer, ed., *Aesthetic Formations*, 9.

[16] For a detailed discussion of such issues, see Schulz, *Muslims and New Media in West Africa*.

[17] Paolo Apolito, *The Internet and the Madonnna: Religious Visionary Experience on the Web*, trans. Anthony Shugaar (Chicago: University of Chicago Press, 2005), 155.

Making the Magal on RTS 1

During the month of Safar, channel 1 of Radiodiffusion Télévision Sénégalaise (RTS 1), Senegal's national television station, prepares its coverage of the Màggal gu Mag. Derived from the Wolof verb *màggal,* meaning "to exalt, praise, or pray to God," and *mag,* meaning "old" or "important," the phrase can be roughly translated as "the great celebration."[18] Known in French as *le Grand Magal*, the event commemorates Amadu Bamba's 1895 exile to Gabon at the hands of the French colonial regime, and is by far the most important celebration in the Murid calendar. Each year, Murid disciples descend upon Touba, the site that was revealed to Bamba in the late 1880s and today acts as the undisputed capital of the Muridiyya. The three-day celebration includes a visit to the city's Great Mosque and the adjacent mausoleum where Bamba is entombed. Pilgrims often visit other sites associated with Bamba's life as well as shrines devoted to Bamba's sons, several of whom have served as caliphs. The Grand Magal also affords an opportunity for disciples to visit their own shaykhs, who either live in Touba year-round or maintain part-time residence. At night, groups of disciples gather for *dhikr* sessions or to chant Amadu Bamba's poems. For three days, Touba is saturated in sacred sound.[19]

During this period, what is normally a city of half a million grows by a few hundred thousand at least, with perhaps one to two million pilgrims "making" the *magal* to Touba each year.[20] With roughly 500,000 inhabitants, Touba is the second most populous city in Senegal after the capital of Dakar, surpassing the coastal city and former colonial capital of Saint-Louis, major train depots such as Thies and Rufisque, and regional capitals such as Kaolack and Ziguinchor. Yet it was only recently that Touba overtook these older urban agglomerations. In 1913, colonial demographers

[18] See the entry for *màggal* in Pamela Munro and Dieynaba Gaye, *Ay Baati Wolof: A Wolof Dictionary,* revised ed., Occasional Papers in Linguistics no. 19 (Los Angeles: University of California at Los Angeles, 1997), 111. The word *magg* also means to make something grow, or to commemorate in a more figurative sense. See Cheikh Anta Babou, "Urbanizing Mystical Islam: Making Murid Space in the Cities of Senegal," *International Journal of African Historical Studies* 40, no. 2 (2007): 199.

[19] For an overview of the event, see Christian Coulon, "The Grand Magal in Touba: A Religious Festival of the Mouride Brotherhood of Senegal," *African Affairs* 98, no. 391 (1999): 195–210.

[20] Eric Ross, *Sufi City: Urban Design and Archetypes in Touba* (Rochester, N.Y.: University of Rochester Press, 2006), 76.

claimed only 500 inhabitants for the town, while Donal B. Cruise O'Brien did not think the population surpassed 3,000 during his stay in the mid-1960s.[21] For many years it was not even included on national maps.[22] What accounts for this complete reversal in fortune? Many explanations have been advanced for the rapid growth of Senegal's cities in the late twentieth century, from the collapse of a cash-crop economy based on peanut exports to the "rural exodus" that resulted from the Sahelian droughts of the early 1970s, and Touba has not been insulated from such developments. It is nevertheless distinguished by its status as the nexus of a far-flung religious order and transnational trade network.

But what is the relation between the coverage of the Grand Magal on RTS 1 and the circulation of Murid videos in the diaspora, in shops like Touba Khassida? As mentioned above, pilgrimage DVDs are one of the most commonly circulating genres of Murid videos, and many pilgrimage DVDs include Magal coverage recorded directly from RTS 1. This does not necessarily mean that they are a faithful and exact reproduction of RTS 1's programming. Indeed, it is clear from the quality of the videos themselves that extensive editing has been done. In any case, the recording of the Grand Magal in the format of a DVD does alter RTS 1's presentation in one paramount way: it renders it perpetually available. Every 18th of Safar, diasporic Murids no longer need to arrange access to a television that receives the channel. Instead, they can experience the Grand Magal year-round with the help of a DVD player.

There is also the question of the videos' content itself. What is one watching when one watches "Magal Touba 2008" or "Grand Magal de Touba 2009 v:1/2," two DVDs that were available for purchase at Touba Khassida in the fall of 2010? At first glance, there does not appear to be any obvious narrative structure to the videos. Instead, one is presented with a series of segments devoted to different aspects of the celebration. The viewer moves from scene to scene—footage of young Murids visiting Amadu Bamba's grave, meetings where prominent shaykhs host and bless their disciples, speeches given by visiting dignitaries—with little sense of the overall picture. However, as the videos progress (an average running time is three to four hours), a particular mode of organization begins to suggest itself.

---

[21] Donal B. Cruise O'Brien, *Symbolic Confrontations: Muslims Imagining the State in Africa* (New York: Palgrave, 2003), 64.

[22] Ross, *Sufi City*, 117.

Different pieces of *magal* coverage—a session with a prominent shaykh, a speech delivered by a visiting Chechen mufti, a tour of Touba's central library—are separated by a panoramic view of Touba's crowded streets. The camera, presumably mounted on a slow-moving vehicle, makes its way through the crowd, the minaret of the Great Mosque centered in the frame, creating a nearly static dolly shot. A few passers-by, usually young men and boys, spot the camera and begin leaping and waving. But for the most part, the people on-screen go about their business and the viewers can simply take in the street scene. It is the closest one comes to the proverbial fly on the wall. Such interludes give the sense of moving through the city, as the viewer observes the various activities that take place during the Grand Magal. Of course, the process of re-creating the pilgrimage in DVD format is not total. A viewer of a *magal* video need not stand in line for long hours waiting to enter the Great Mosque. Nor does one sit in crowded public transportation attempting to get from one part of the city to another (though one DVD of the 2009 *magal* does begin with a lengthy montage of pilgrims arriving in Touba on jets, trains, buses, trucks, and horse-drawn carts). But many of the more mundane aspects of the pilgrimage are indeed represented for extended periods: scenes of people waiting, talking on cell phones, setting up tables and chairs. In many pilgrimage DVDs, food preparation earns extended screen-time.

In addition to tableaus of Touba's streets and kitchens, recordings of *dhikr* sessions are used to separate individual scenes. These normally continue for several minutes (and the sessions themselves are known to go on for several hours). As is well known, *dhikr* is performed in many places of the Islamic world, and has been the subject of research for many scholars of Islam, especially those concerned with its bodily and sensory aspects.[23] The practice of *dhikr* recitation, or what Ibn ʿAta' Allah deemed *dhikr* of the tongue (which he distinguished from *dhikr* of the heart and "secret" *dhikr*),[24] is a particularly visible and auditory element of Murid practice. What is notable in DVDs of the Grand Magal is that no single

[23] *Dhikr* appears in several different bodies of scholarship within anthropology and Islamic studies. For an anthropological treatment, see Jonathan H. Shannon, "The Aesthetics of Spiritual Practice and the Creation of Moral and Musical Subjectivities in Aleppo, Syria," *Ethnology* 43, no. 4 (2004): 381–91. For a view from Islamic studies, see Richard J. A. McGregor, "A Sufi Legacy in Tunis: Prayer and the Shadhiliyya," *International Journal of Middle East Studies* 29, no. 2 (1997): 255–77.

[24] McGregor, "A Sufi Legacy in Tunis," 267.

stock footage is used to portray such practices. Instead, sessions are differentiated, with some recitation leaders introduced by snippets of biographical information. In addition to individual prayer leaders and the contents of the different prayers themselves, visual cues also separate one *dhikr* session from the next. It is clear from the footage, for example, that sessions take place at different times of day.

Though *dhikr* sessions are numerous in *magal* DVDs, it is probably reductive to think of them as merely "dividing" more "substantive" sections of the videos. After all, *dhikr* sessions probably comprise a larger percentage of the running time of pilgrimage DVDs than any other activity. Altogether, the first disc of a two-disc DVD set for the Grand Magal of 2009 clocks in at just over four hours. With the entire celebration lasting only three days, it is safe to say that the length of many *magal* DVDs, if purchased and viewed in their entirety (some are multiple volumes), approaches a significant proportion of the duration of the Grand Magal itself. With the alternation of *dhikr* sessions and street scenes marking the *magal* procession, and accompanied by visual cues indicating the succession of days and nights, one possible logic of the DVD's structure becomes apparent: it mimics the format of the pilgrimage itself.

Also lending the proceedings some sense of structure—and reminding the viewer that one is indeed watching a DVD and not physically traveling to Touba itself—is the voiced-over narration of two presenters, Serigne Moustapha Mbacké Gueye and Serigne Moustapha Diattara. Together, they provide elucidatory commentary and give thanks and recognition to the specific figures on-screen, such as particularly notable shaykhs or different *dhikr* leaders. They also narrate the filmed visitations of different sites associated with the memory of Amadu Bamba. Footage from a DVD of the 2009 Grand Magal shows Murids visiting a village outside of Touba, which Diattara and Gueye inform the viewer to be Mbacké Barry Dioloff, the point of departure for Bamba's exile from Touba. The video then moves to Louga, a larger town that Bamba passed through on the way to Saint-Louis, where he was finally exiled from Senegal. In this manner the DVD presents a clear historical narrative that provides a trajectory for the pilgrimage itself (or its consumption in video format).

Historicizing the Grand Magal

Murid pilgrimage videos are both components of religious practice and acts of historicization. In fact, the very creation of Murid space is often achieved through the revision of historical narratives, rendering historicization an important aspect of religious practice itself. As noted above, many segments of pilgrimage videos are devoted to the recounting of the history of Bamba's exile in Gabon. Bamba was permitted to return to Senegal in 1902, seven years after his initial expulsion (a length of time weighted with numerological significance), only to be exiled again a year later, this time to neighboring Mauritania, where he had previously studied and taken the *wird* of the Qadiriyya. He returned to settle permanently in Senegal in 1907 and was relocated in 1912 to the town of Diourbel, where he oversaw the expansion of *dar al-Murid* until his death in 1927. This basic historical narrative is well known and often conveyed in pilgrimage videos. Through such sequences, these videos serve not only to re-create the religious experience of the Grand Magal, but to illustrate the experience of Bamba's exile. The two narratives are in fact inextricable since, strictly speaking, the Grand Magal commemorates Bamba's departure. By drawing a direct line between the pilgrim and the historic exile of a saint, Murid pilgrimage DVDs incorporate the transcendent into the very process of historicization itself. This process is centered on narratives of travel and return. In other words, the institution of the Grand Magal—the perpetuation of "structures and behaviors connected with the assertion and maintenance of religious authority," to cite the words of one recent overview of Islamic institutions[25]—is rooted in experiences of exile and distance.

The first celebration of Bamba's exile occurred in 1912, when he was under house arrest in the town of Diourbel. Following Bamba's death in 1927, his body was buried in Touba, a posthumous return to the holy site after two periods of exile and an extended house arrest. Soon after, his son and the first Murid caliph, Mamadu Mustafa, marked his father's exile with an event in Touba, and it was soon recast as an annual celebration of the Muridiyya.[26] Disciples came not only to take part in the pilgrimage, but to help build the new city. The construction of Touba's Great Mosque,

[25] Joseph E. Lowry, "Institution," in *Key Themes for the Study of Islam*, ed. Jamal J. Elias (Oxford: Oneworld, 2010), 201.

[26] Cheikh Anta Babou, *Fighting the Greater Jihad: Amadu Bamba and the Founding of the Muridiyya, 1853–1913* (Athens: Ohio University Press, 2007), 167, 256 n. 24. According to Coulon, the date of the Grand Magal originally marked Bamba's death. Only in 1946 was it changed to coincide with the anniversary of his exile to Gabon. See Coulon, "The Grand Magal," 200.

whose minaret is sometimes claimed to be the tallest in sub-Saharan Africa, began in 1931 and took decades to finish. During that time, innumerable pilgrims contributed to construction efforts, which were finally completed in 1963.

Around the same time, the first moving images of the Magal were produced. *Le Grand Magal de Touba* (1961) has much in common with contemporary pilgrimage videos. Both are as much auditory as visual experience. Prayer recitation accompanies an early montage of different views of the city. Pilgrims are then shown arriving in trains, buses, and cars. As in many contemporary pilgrimage videos, food preparation and consumption are depicted at length in *Le Grand Magal de Touba.* Clips from the film can be viewed on YouTube, and according to its entry in the Internet Movie Database, the director Blaise Senghor was awarded the Silver Bear in the category of short film at the Berlin International Film Festival for his efforts.[27]

The history of the Grand Magal is intertwined with the history of Touba itself. As mentioned above, the expansion of the city and the Muridiyya's relationship with the Senegalese state have in many ways shaped the practice of the pilgrimage. Since 1976, Touba's official legal status has been that of an "autonomous rural community," but such terminology only formalized a relationship that had long been in place. Even the French colonial state had recognized Touba as a "collective private domain." For most of its existence, Touba's basic civil institutions have been under the authority of the caliph, not the state. The Grand Magal therefore proceeds beyond the reach of state networks, and any participation on the part of the state is usually aimed at currying favor with influential shaykhs. Other *magals* have expanded beyond the realm of *dar al-Murid,* however, into other cities in Senegal where Murids are not the majority and where state approval for public celebrations is required. Such *magals* have also been the subject of pilgrimage videos.

The Magal of Two Rakkas

Of all the lesser *magals,* one of the most widely attended is the Magal of Two Rakkas in Saint-Louis. Unlike the Grand Magal, which commemorates Bamba's exile, this *magal* celebrates what some Murid disciples interpret as Bamba's defiance of French authorities when he was detained in the city before being transported to Gabon. Once again, a clue to the

[27] The first 10 minutes of the 25-minute film can be viewed at http://www.youtube.com/watch?v=7k0_7NYqE6A.

historical moment that the celebration recognizes is to be found in the event's name. The Wolof word *ràkk* (or *ràkka*) is an Arabic loan word (from *raʿka*) that refers to a "complete act of praying" in which "one stands up, recites a verse from the Koran, bows halfway, stands again, kneels, and touches one's head to the ground."[28] The particular act of prayer that constitutes the reference point for Saint-Louis's *magal* occurred when Amadu Bamba was detained by French authorities in the colonial governor's residence in 1895. During his detention, Bamba recited the prayer of two *rakkas*—a shortened prayer that, according to one interpretation, Bamba performed at moments of danger when he was unable to complete a full prayer of three to four genuflections.[29] It is this act that is celebrated, with the outstanding moment of the pilgrimage coming when Murids gather in the central square of Saint-Louis and collectively reenact Bamba's prayer.

The Magal of Two Rakkas takes place every September 5 and thus, unlike the Grand Magal, its celebration is tied to the Christian calendar. It is of much more recent advent than the Grand Magal, having been established independently of caliphal authority by Madické Wade in 1976 (it soon obtained official approval). Much smaller than its counterpart in Touba, the Magal of Two Rakkas still attract tens of thousands of pilgrims each year. Pont Faidherbe, the bridge that leads to Saint-Louis (which is situated on an island), is closed to motorized traffic and people must cross the bridge on foot. One important part of the *magal* is a visit to the cell in the former governor's residence where Bamba was kept during his imprisonment. Today, it is a shrine dedicated to the shaykh and Murids visit it in order to acknowledge a pivotal moment in Bamba's life. While certainly not on the same scale as the Grand Magal, the Magal of Two Rakkas has carved out a place for itself on the Murid calendar.[30]

It has likewise carved a place for itself in the world of Murid pilgrimage videos. But unlike the DVDs of the Grand Magal discussed above, *Magal des 2 Rakaa 1998* (the name of one Saint-Louis pilgrimage video available at Touba Khassida in Little Senegal) does not consist of recorded footage from Senegalese television. Instead, it gives the appearance of a more modest, internal affair. As the opening shot of the video indicates, it was produced by "Baghdad Audio←→Video," which is based in

[28] Munro and Gaye, *Ay Baati Wolof: A Wolof Dictionary,* 161.

[29] Babou, "Urbanizing Mystical Islam," 200.

[30] See Ferdinand de Jong, "Remembering the Nation: The Murid Maggal of St. Louis, Senegal," *Cahiers d'Études Africaines* 197 (2010): 123–51.

Zingonia, a town in the commune of Bergamo about 40 kilometers outside of Milan in Italy.[31] This very first frame of text eventually fades out to reveal the edges of a painting, then the contours of a white robe, and finally Amadu Bamba's face. Then there is another cut to "Baghdad Audio←→Video," followed by a collage of Bamba, his son and Murid caliph Serigne Saliou Mbacké, and pictures of various mosques. The introductory announcement begins as the camera focuses on a black-and-white painting of men in pith helmets leading a figure in a white robe (surely Bamba himself) to a ship waiting in a harbor. So concludes the opening to *Magal des 2 Rakaa 1998*.

Like the videos of the Grand Magal, the video of the Magal of Two Rakkas also rehearses the major points of Amadu Bamba's life, centering on his time in Saint-Louis and his subsequent exile to Gabon. The Murid capital, though constantly evoked in prayer and speeches, also plays a much smaller role in the video's economy of images, with greater attention paid to Saint-Louis. Many of the activities presented in the video, such as speeches given by prominent Murid shaykhs and sessions of *dhikr,* resemble those found in videos of the Grand Magal. Gone, however, are the choreographed performances of foreign ambassadors and state representatives.[32] It appears to be an event of purely regional scope, less concerned with recognition from outsiders, be they non-Murids or Murids from the diaspora. The role of Arabic is reduced as well, with practically all of the prayers and speeches given in Wolof.

Though Bamba himself is still very much the focus of the video, many of Bamba's early disciples are also examined at length in *Magal des 2 Rakaa 1998*. One of them, Serigne Cheikh Abdourahmane Lo (also known as Ndaam Abdrahman Lo), is the subject of numerous interventions. A black-and-white head shot of Lo is visible throughout much of video, as different shaykhs take turns giving accounts of his life and his service to the Muridiyya. Lo was one of the Muridiyya's earliest disciples who was not a member of Bamba's family. While Bamba was in exile in Gabon, Lo directed a school and taught the Qur'an to many of the order's early disciples, including several of Bamba's sons.[33] He is thus remembered as someone who ensured the order's

---

[31] When the DVD was produced in 1998 Italy had a Senegalese population of 35,000, most of whom were Murids. See Bruno Riccio, "From Ethnic Group to Transnational Community? Senegalese Migrants' Ambivalent Experiences and Multiple Trajectories," *Journal of Ethnic and Migration Studies* 27, no. 4 (2001): 584.

[32] This observation is based on a DVD of the 1998 Magal of Two Rakkas. It has been reported that the heads of five government ministries attended in 2004, suggesting that the event is growing in importance. See de Jong, "Remembering the Nation," 141.

[33] Babou, *Fighting the Greater Jihad,* 103.

survival while its leader was in exile. Much as the Magal of Two Rakkas establishes Murid celebrations in cities outside of the capital of Touba, so does it create space for other figures in the history of the order to be remembered.

To a much greater extent than other Murid events, the Magal of Two Rakkas concerns itself with Senegal's colonial history. According to one popular version of the story of Bamba's imprisonment in Saint-Louis, all of Senegal's marabouts were summoned to Saint-Louis, where it was demanded that they renounce Islam. Only Bamba refused, reciting the famous two prayers that led to his exile. Such a narrative bolsters Bamba's anticolonial credentials while diminishing those of non-Murid Muslims, thereby rewriting Bamba as a figure without whom Senegal might still be under foreign rule and Islam might still be repressed.[34] In this manner, the prominence of the Muridiyya in present-day Senegal is written back into the country's historical narrative. And just as the Magal of Two Rakkas changes history, it transforms space with the spread of celebrations to other cities in Senegal. Ceremonies near the port of Dakar are now performed to celebrate Bamba's return from exile.[35] Murids have searched for other sites where Amadu Bamba may have sojourned. The creation of Murid space is ongoing, and nowhere has it been more active than in the growing Murid diaspora overseas.

The Diaspora Online and on Film

The proliferation of Murid videos is premised on the notion that one can effect spiritual communion through the medium of film, and it is this notion that clarifies their utility (both potential and realized) in a far-flung religious network, which some scholars have even termed a diaspora.[36] That said, the foregoing typology of videos provides no concrete evidence of how such material is actually used. Up to this point, any analysis touching on that question has largely been extrapolated from the content of the videos themselves. But do Murids really sit down and attentively watch

[34] This popular Murid historiography is presented in de Jong, "Remembering the Nation," 134.
[35] Babou, "Urbanizing Mystical Islam," 209.
[36] See Mamadou Diouf, "The Senegalese Murid Trade Diaspora and the Making of a Vernacular Cosmopolitanism," *Public Culture* 12, no. 3 (2000): 679–702. For more restricted conceptualizations of diaspora, see Khachig Tölölyan, "The Contemporary Discourse of Diaspora Studies," *Comparative Studies of South Asia, Africa and the Middle East* 27, no. 3 (2007): 647–55.

footage of *magals*? Do such videos require the undivided attention of a submissive audience in order for them to do their work? Or could they simply be allowed to play in the background while "viewers" go about their business, not needing to view (and read) such videos in any particular way? Such questions suggest an alternative understanding of videos not as bearers of meanings that need to be decoded, but as agentive objects in their own right. Gregory Starrett has alluded to the protective potential of copies of the Qur'an not as text, but as material objects themselves, which explains why he so often found them stored in velvet boxes in the back windows of cars in Cairo, their protective shrink-wrap still intact.[37] Could a similar logic also apply to Murid pilgrimage DVDs?

In order to sketch out how one would begin answering this question, it may be helpful to think of these DVDs not only as media, but as art objects in the sense that Alfred Gell gave the term. In his attempt at producing an anthropological theory of art, Gell widened the notion of art, denoting art objects "indexes of agency": "the anthropology of art . . . is just anthropology itself, except that it deals with those situations in which there is an 'index of agency' which is normally some kind of artefact."[38] In Gell's terms, the index is the material manifestation of a prototype and, as such, can take many different forms, from iconic images of the Virgin to sculpted idols. It can even be a person, as is the case in bodily possession by a spirit or deity. The inclusion of people is in fact crucial for Gell because it dissolves the distinction between performance and artifacts.

As the category of "art object" expands, one may be left wondering if nearly anything could be made to fall within its capacious boundaries. *Art and Agency* does not dwell on this point in any detail, but it is recognized that although "crude and uninteresting artefacts . . . fall within the scope of the anthropology of art they have no significance as 'works of art,' because *nobody attends to their making as a particularly salient feature of their agency*."[39] Seemingly in passing, Gell pinpoints the creative process itself (the act of "making," whether the product in question is an object or performance) as the decisive characteristic that distinguishes his anthropology of art from anthropology at large. It is this point that orients us towards a sense of how videos are used in contemporary religious practice.

---

[37] Gregory Starrett, "The Political Economy of Religious Commodities in Cairo," *American Anthropologist* 97, no. 1 (1995): 53.

[38] Alfred Gell, *Art and Agency: An Anthropological Theory* (Oxford: Clarendon, 1998), 66.

[39] Ibid., 68, emphasis added.

Understandings of Murid videos and the work that they do will undoubtedly benefit from a more detailed knowledge of how these videos are produced, the material conditions of their production and distribution, and the skills and techniques employed by their creators. It may also shed light on the debates and contestations that attend this kind of cultural production. Cheikh Guèye has, in a general manner, alluded to the politics behind television coverage of the Grand Magal. The selection of shaykhs to televise and initiatives to highlight (as well as the necessary omissions and exclusions entailed by these choices) form part of the Muridiyya's "communication strategy," an "audiovisual dream" that is now being realized by Murid television stations like Lamp Fall Television and Touba TV.[40] Examining the processes behind DVD production and circulation elaborates Guèye's general claim. It also addresses the concern that studies of Murid visual practice tend to depoliticize their subject matter, presenting a realm of cultural production free of any substantial debate or disagreement.[41] With respect to DVDs, to "attend to their making," as Gell would have us do, is to have a great understanding of their practical use and political implications.

In addition to illustrating the ways in which new media inflect religious practice, videos will also continue to inform us about a religious community that has expanded beyond the groups of itinerant traders that first attracted academic attention in the late 1980s and early 1990s.[42] Just as videos transmit images of Touba to dispersed disciples, they can also depict the figurative and physical expansion of Murid frontiers far from the Murid homeland, beyond the well-known Senegalese neighborhoods of New York and Marseille to cities like Baltimore, Memphis, and Winston-Salem. In each of these locations, the establishment of associations known as *dahiras* has entailed the production of Murid space through the purchase of homes that act as meeting places and residences for visiting shaykhs (Keur Serigne Touba, or House of the Master of

[40] Cheikh Guèye, "Enjeux et rôles des NTIC dans les mutations urbaines: Le cas de Touba," in *Le Sénégal à l'heure de l'information: Tecnologies et société,* ed. Momar-Coumba Diop (Paris: Karthala, 2002), 175–76.

[41] See in particular Benjamin F. Soares, "Rethinking Islam and Muslim Societies in Africa," *African Affairs* 106, no. 423 (2007): 319–26.

[42] See Victoria Ebin, "Camelots à New York, les pionniers de l'immigration sénégalaise," *Hommes et Migrations* 1160 (1992): 32–37; Victoria Ebin, "Making Room versus Creating Space: The Construction of Spatial Categories by Itinerant Mouride Traders," in *Making Muslim Space in North America and Europe,* ed. Barbara Metcalf (Berkeley: University of California Press, 1996); Scott L. Malcomson, "West of Eden," *Transition* 71 (1996): 26–45.

Touba).[43] Videos depicting the inauguration of a new *dahira* or the visit of a particularly prominent shaykh form part of what Ousmane Kane recently termed "the transnational spiritual economy," a sphere of movement and exchange of persons and goods that characterizes Senegalese communities in the United States.[44]

Much as pilgrimage videos allow dispersed communities of Murids to retain a link to Touba, videos addressing Murid expansion also serve to propagate the image of Amadu Bamba to new localities. As it turns out, Alfred Gell's concept of distributed personhood, his notion that "we are present not just in our single bodies, but in everything in our surroundings which bears witness to our existence, our attributes, and our agency," finds a neat illustration in a recent report on RTS 1 about the continuing peregrinations of the Murid founder.[45] The subject of the report was the Murid *dahira* of Memphis, Tennessee, whose secretary general Khadim Samb gave an account of his organization's plan to build a mosque and Keur Serigne Touba in the hometown of Elvis Presley. During his interview, Samb explicitly invoked the King and his relation to the Murid saint: "If Memphis is on the rise today, it's because of Elvis Presley . . . Shaykh Amadu Bamba is in the middle of this and that simply confirms what he said: 'one day I will be everywhere in the world.'"[46] Like the spread of *dahiras,* videos are one of Bamba's vehicles for being "everywhere in the world." They provide a particular method of mediating his disciples' spiritual lives and social relations, whether in Touba or in the American South. And in increasingly heated debates over the visibility of Muslim practice in the United States, when the prospect of building a mosque in downtown Manhattan is in many quarters viewed as an existential threat, it is worth recognizing that in Samb's view, the "Americanization" of the Muridiyya is not incompatible with the "Muridization" of Memphis.

---

[43] For a video report on the growth of the *dahira* of Baltimore, see www.youtube.com/watch?v=fzCERgrN1RU&feature=related. In general, *dahiras* strive to maintain Murid practices abroad by consolidating resources that facilitate the performance of pilgrimages, marriages, baptisms, and even the repatriation of deceased Murid disciples to cemeteries in Touba. See Cheikh Anta Babou, "Brotherhood Solidarity, Education and Migration: The Role of *Dahiras* Among the Murid Muslim Community of New York," *African Affairs* 101 (2002): 151–70.

[44] See chap. 5 of Ousmane Oumar Kane, *The Homeland Is the Arena: Religion, Transnationalism, and the Integration of Senegalese Immigrants in America* (Oxford: Oxford University Press, 2011).

[45] Gell, *Art and Agency*, 103.

[46] www.youtube.com/watch?v=JayshRMG5EE&feature=related, 0:43-1:05.

Pilgrimage Through Poetry: Sung Journeys Within the Murid Spiritual Diaspora

*Christine Thu Nhi Dang,** UNIVERSITY OF PENNSYLVANIA

DOI: 10.5192/21540993040169

ABSTRACT

This study examines the role of musical tradition in unifying the spiritual itineraries of a globalized religious community. Within the Muridiyya, an important Senegalese Sufi order, the singing of Arabic poetry written by Shaykh Ahmadu Bamba is a fundamental rite of sacred journeys, the most notable of which is the annual pilgrimage to the holy city of Touba. At the heart of this pilgrimage is the story of Bamba's departure on exile, a foundational story powerfully evoked in the singing of the shaykh's poetry. For Murids in diasporic communities distant from Senegal, the singing of sacred poetry can become a compelling substitute for ritual travel to Touba. Through sung poetry, believers in the widespread Murid diaspora can fulfill a sonic pilgrimage, an acoustic homecoming, a metaphysical return to their beloved spiritual home.

I am grateful to Mbacké Thioune and the Dahira Moukhadimatoul Khidma of Philadelphia for introducing me to the *magal.* I am indebted to Hizbut-Tarqiyyah and its Moral Responsible Serigne Atou Diagne for their hospitality and valuable aid in research during the *magal* of 2012. I thank Papa Assane Diouf, of the International Institute for Studies and Research on Muridism, for deepening my understanding of Bamba's poetry; Monique Ingalls, for influencing my thinking on musical journeys; and Cheikh Anta Babou, for tremendously helping me in the expansion and publication of this work. Finally, I thank Timothy Rommen for his steadfast support throughout this project.

Islamic Africa, VOL. 4, NO. 1, 2013. ISSN 2154-0993. www.islamicafricajournal.org

February 3, 2010. On the eve of a winter storm, as the snow began to accumulate on the frozen ground, nearly seventy Senegalese immigrants gathered in the banquet room of a Philadelphia motel to celebrate with prayer and poetry and food their most important religious event. Dressed in long, regal robes tailored from lustrous, richly dyed fabric, they would spend the evening sharing piquant Senegalese dishes and drinking spicy, black herbal coffee, while ritually re-immersing in the founding stories and sounds of their faith. In the middle of that sparsely filled banquet room, eight men sat barefoot in a circle on the floor around open hymnbooks, exuberantly and loudly singing religious poetry in Arabic, their voices in volume and richness suggesting more performers than were actually there. Those men and women not directly involved in the singing swayed from side to side in their chairs, snapped their fingers, tapped their feet, and joined in the verses from time to time—their spontaneous contributions thickening the vocal layers of the primary singers, the emergent antiphonal texture imparting to the Arabic verses a heightened rhythmic impetus and an insistent sensation of pulse. At times, individuals stood to show their delight in the singing. At times, they exclaimed expressions of deep pleasure. At times, there was dancing. There they would rest from early evening until dawn, the impassioned tones of sung poetry and the thick aroma of spicy coffee inundating that motel banquet room to such an extent as to make one forget, momentarily, the severity of that long Philadelphia winter and the urgency of the impending northeastern storm.

Those present in that motel banquet room were Muslims belonging to the Muridiyya, a Sufi order that counts more than four million members within and without Senegal.[1] The poems or *qaṣāʾid* that they sang were written by Ahmadu Bamba, the beloved founder of the Muridiyya. And the event for which they gathered on that cold winter night was the Grand Magal—the annual pilgrimage commanded of the faithful to Touba, the holy city of the Muridiyya in Senegal. As those Murids in Philadelphia could not physically undertake the pilgrimage to welcome the Grand Magal, they gathered in that motel banquet room instead, to reproduce the sacred poems that—at that very moment—were loudly reverberating in Touba, throughout Senegal, and across the wide reach of the Murid diaspora. On

[1] In 2005, Cheikh Anta Babou estimated the worldwide Murid population to be roughly four million; see Cheikh Anta Babou, *Fighting the Greater Jihad: Amadu Bamba and the Founding of the Muridiyya of Senegal, 1853–1913* (Athens: Ohio University Press, 2007), 193 n. 4.

the day of the Grand Magal, the striking tones of Bamba's *qaṣāʾid* radiate from the spiritual heart of Touba to Murid communities in Europe, North America, the Middle East, and Asia—generating a musically coherent yet spatially diffused diasporic soundscape of faith.

This is a study about sacred journeys, self-imposed exile, and spiritual community, and the ways in which they are mediated and linked through singing. I begin by discussing the significance of Touba as a center of spiritual assemblage, a destination of pilgrimage that draws to itself traveling believers seeking to imbibe its *baraka,* to absorb its blessedness. I then introduce the history of Bamba's sacred poems, focusing on the remarkable culture of singing that has emerged in their performance. Fundamental to contemporary Murid identity, the singing of sacred poetry is essential in promoting unity and reaffirming belonging, given the challenges confronting the globalized, diasporized Sufi community. For Murids dispersed abroad, the singing of Bamba's poems can produce and maintain a vital connection to the religious center, even when that center has become physically inaccessible. Poetic performance can become a metonym for both the physical place of Touba and for ritual pilgrimage to Touba—enacting powerful experiences of collective return to geographic, cultural, and spiritual roots. When displaced believers cannot go to Touba, they sing a metaphoric pilgrimage through sacred poetry instead.[2]

Based on research with Murid communities in Philadelphia during the *magals* of 2010 and 2011 and in Senegal during the *magal* of 2012, this study highlights the extent to which the distinct sounds of Bamba's sung verses contribute acoustically to believers' perceptions of the event's extraordinariness. Poetic performance connects the individual and collective,

[2] The Grand Magal of Touba and other Murid *magals* have been examined in a number of interesting articles. This study contributes to this existing literature by focusing on singing and poetry, prominent aspects of *magals* that have not been explored. See Amar Samb, "Touba et son 'Magal,'" *Bulletin de l'IFAN* (Dakar) 31 (1969): 733–53; Leonardo A. Villalón, "Sufi Rituals as Rallies: Religious Ceremonies in the Politics of Senegalese State-Society Relations," *Comparative Politics* 26, no. 4 (1994): 415–37; Christian Coulon, "The Grand Magal in Touba: A Religious Festival of the Mouride Brotherhood of Senegal," *African Affairs* 98, no. 391 (1999): 195–210; Sophie Bava and Cheikh Guèye, "Le grand magal de Touba: Exil prophétique, migration et pèlerinage au sein du mouridisme," *Social Compass* 48, no. 3 (2001): 421–38; Cheikh Anta Babou, "Urbanizing Mystical Islam: Making Murid Space in the Cities of Senegal," *International Journal of African Historical Studies* 40, no. 2 (2007): 197–223; Ferdinand de Jong, "Remembering the Nation: The Murid Maggal in Saint Louis, Senegal," *Cahiers d'Études Africaines* 197 (2010): 123–51.

historical and contemporary, foundational and circumstantial stories of faithful exile that are evoked during the Grand Magal. Poetry—fervently sung at the top of the lungs—is the privileged mechanism that makes the diasporic imaginaries and multi-sited itineraries of pilgrimage to Touba ideologically, and somatically, possible.

The Place of Touba

Travel becomes sacred journey when it is undertaken, with purpose, towards a place of spiritual significance. To constitute a destination of sacred journey, this place must be more than mere geographic site. This place must also enclose a sanctified entity of historical time, enfolding within itself a unique narrative central to the identity of the religious community. Acts of mimesis, acts of displacement and time-travel, sacred journeys are fundamentally acts of imagination that conduct traveling feet to those extraordinary, consecrated, and spiritually irreplaceable places where the presence of the divine is felt here on earth.

The holy city of Touba in the heart of Senegal is such a place for disciples of the Muridiyya. It was in Touba that Shaykh Ahmadu Bamba Mbacké founded the Muridiyya in 1887.[3] According to Murid tradition, Bamba was divinely led to a large tree where Touba stands today. Underneath this tree, Bamba entered a mystic state of knowing in which it was revealed that he would establish upon that site a pious community. This community would rehabilitate the authentic path of Islam, the original way demarcated and adhered to by the Prophet and his companions. Bamba named this site Touba, meaning "bliss" or "felicity," directly after the mention of the word in the Qur'an: "Those who believe and do righteous deeds, bliss (*ṭūbā*) is theirs, and a beautiful place of return."[4]

It is believed that verses of Bamba's poem, *Maṭlab al-fawzayn* (*The*

---

[3] For more on the history of the Muridiyya and the founding of Touba, see Cheikh Tidiane Sy, *La confrérie sénégalaise des mourides* (Paris: Presence africaine, 1969); Donal Cruise O'Brien, *The Mourides of Senegal: The Political and Economic Organization of an Islamic Brotherhood* (London: Oxford University Press, 1971); Jean Copans, *Les marabouts de l'arachide* (Paris: L'Harmattan, 1988); David Robinson, *Paths of Accommodation; Muslim Societies and French Colonial Authorities in Senegal and Mauritania, 1880–1920* (Athens: Ohio University Press, 2000); and Cheikh Anta Babou, *Fighting the Greater Jihad: Amadu Bamba and the Founding of the Muridiyya of Senegal, 1853–1913* (Athens: Ohio University Press, 2007).

[4] Qur'an 13:29.

Quest for Happiness in the Two Worlds), were composed the moment Bamba first set foot on the holy site. *Maṭlab al-fawzayn* remains the first and final word on the origin, character, and destiny of the city—leading Cheikh Guèye to aptly label it a "foundational poem" that represents the birth certificate of Touba.[5] In *Maṭlab al-fawzayn,* Bamba depicts Touba as a liminal space where the spiritual world and the carnal world converge, a felicitous place where the blessings of God can be experienced and known ever more intensely. Bamba writes, "Make my abode the blessed city of Touba, the preferred citadel of Allah and the Prophet (may peace be upon him) here on earth, where we dwell."[6] Bamba envisions Touba as a sanctuary for complete submission to Islam, a refuge from the tumults of the outside world. "Make my abode the blessed city of Touba, a place where one abandons the darkness in order to enter into the light, protect this city from the disgraced."[7] Bamba asserts the ultimate kinship of Touba and Mecca—insisting that journey to Touba can bestow the same spiritual rewards as the hajj or obligatory pilgrimage to the most sacred city of the Muslim world. Bamba writes, "Make my abode the blessed city of Touba, a place that gives the charismatic rewards of the hajj to he who wishes to undertake it but is indigent and unable to go to Mecca."[8]

In Wolof, Ahmadu Bamba is devotedly called by followers "Serigne Touba," the holy man of Touba. It is in Touba that the Grand Mosque of the Muridiyya, the mausoleum of Bamba and his sons, the wells of mercy holding sanctified water, and other monuments said to be brimming with the *baraka* of Murid saints are located.[9] Currently the second largest city in Senegal, Touba's rapid development, burgeoning institutions, and expanding infrastructures—funded by the voluntary labor and financial contributions of devoted believers—attest to the vitality of the Murid faith. As one disciple states, "Touba is the most beautiful city in Senegal, and Serigne Touba is the reason."[10]

---

[5] Cheikh Guèye, *Touba: La capitale des mourides* (Paris: Karthala, 2002), 83. Guèye's well-documented work is the most comprehensive study of Touba, its history, its communities, and its contemporary identity.

[6] Ahmadu Bamba Mbacké, *Maṭlab al-fawzayn* (Dakar: Imprimerie Serigne Issa Niang, n.d.), 13. For a performance of the poem in its entirety, see Serigne Abdou Diouf, *Maṭlab al-fawzayn,* http://www.youtube.com/watch?v=DN6KeKJDboo.

[7] *Maṭlab al-fawzayn,* 14.

[8] *Maṭlab al-fawzayn,* 12.

[9] For a thorough study of Touba's urban geography and its meanings, see Eric Ross, *Sufi City: Urban Design and Archetypes in Touba* (Rochester, N.Y.: University of Rochester Press, 2006).

[10] Khabane Wade, interview with author, Touba, January 10, 2012.

Physical journey to Touba is a recommendation for Murids, just as pilgrimage to Mecca is a required pillar of worship for Muslims. And the time when journey to the city is most advised is during the annual celebration of the Grand Magal, on the 18th day of the Muslim month of Safar. The Grand Magal falls on the anniversary of the first departure of Ahmadu Bamba into exile, which the French colonial government ordered out of fear of the growing authority of the shaykh.[11] On September 21, 1895 (18 Safar 1313H), Bamba left Dakar on a ship heading for imprisonment in Gabon, where he would remain for seven years. In 1912 Bamba pronounced an *ndigal* or religious order that all Murids celebrate his departure into exile as a practice of faith: "For the blessings that God has bestowed upon me, my gratitude alone can no longer repay. Therefore, I invite each person who delights in my personal happiness to unite with me in thanksgiving to God, at each occasion of the anniversary of my departure."[12] In calling all Murids to celebration on the 18th of Safar, Bamba ritualized the collective performance of memory of and gratitude for God's grace during his deportation. Bamba would celebrate the *magal* every year during his stay in Diourbel until his death in 1927.[13]

Murids use the Wolof word *magal* to designate commemorations in which believers journey to spiritually significant places within the history of the Sufi order. In Wolof, *magal* literally means to make something grow—from which the general meaning of the word, to commemorate or celebrate, is derived. The etymology of the word demonstrates a linguistic connection between the idea of sacred journeys and that of memory—particularly of shared memories that increase in importance over time. To *magal* is to call into remembrance a key moment from the sacred past, to preserve this moment through celebration—and in so doing, to make this moment grow in the present and for the future. In Murid culture, the way to make grow critical yet ephemeral events of the past is to gather in the places in which these events became manifest.

[11] Cheikh Anta Babou provides the most complete sociohistorical account of the Gabon exile; see Babou, *Fighting the Greater Jihad,* 115–40.

[12] Recounted in the sermon of Serigne Abdoul Ahad Mbacké, caliph-general, before the *magal* of 1979, debut of Safar 1399H, Touba.

[13] In 1927, Serigne Moustapha Mbacké, Bamba's son and successor, changed the date of the *magal* to correspond with the anniversary of his father's death, and commanded the faithful to converge on this date in Touba. In 1946 the second caliph, Serigne Fallilou Mbacké, changed the date back to the anniversary of the Gabon departure on the 18th of Safar. For more on the sociohistorical contexts in which the *magal* was first recommended, see Babou, *Fighting the Greater Jihad,* 162–74.

Currently attracting more than three million participants annually, the Grand Magal of Touba is a national holiday, the largest celebration—religious or otherwise—within Senegal, and one of the most popular pilgrimages in the world.[14] Prime-time coverage dedicated to the life of Bamba and the history of the Sufi order airs beginning three weeks in advance, and *magal*-related reports dominate newspapers, radio, and television during the week of the event. During this time, travelers from within Senegal can spend up to twenty hours in overcrowded vehicles that descend upon the one road leading to Touba—packing into every available space, piling on top of old buses and rundown minivans driven by sleep-deprived chauffeurs. The 2012 edition of the *magal* recorded at least 15 deaths and 301 injured in traffic accidents on the road to Touba.[15] These perennial dangers, however, do not deter most Murids from doing all that is possible to make it to Touba for the *magal*.

Those living in diasporic communities distant from Senegal also go to great lengths to fulfill the recommendation of journey to Touba. During the Grand Magal, Touba hosts returning Murid emigrants from across the globe. Entrees by Senegalese nationals at the airport increase up to 200 percent in the three months before the event.[16] In the words of Donald Martin Carter, "The world of Mouridism in immigration is vast and extends from the holy city of Touba in Senegal to the major cities of Africa, Europe, the United States, Italy, Spain, France, Germany, Japan, Canada, and Australia: New York, Atlanta, Los Angeles, Turin, Livorno, Milan, Rome, Paris, Toulon, Lyon, Hong Kong, Berlin, London, Yaoundé, and Madrid."[17] During the Grand Magal, many of these regions are represented

[14] An estimated 3.1 million people attended the 2011 edition of the Grand Magal; see Emergence Consulting, "Étude monographique sur l'impact socio-economique du Grand Magal de Touba," directed by Moubarack Lo, Dakar, November 2011, 37.

[15] Samba Khary Ndiaye, "Magal Touba 2012: Macabre bilan de la route: 301 victimes et 15 morts," *rewmi.com,* January 13, 2012, http://www.rewmi.com/Magal-Touba-2012-Macabre-bilan-de-la-route-301-victimes-et-15-morts_a55007.html.

[16] Emergence Consulting, "Étude monographique sur l'impact socio-economique du Grand Magal," 54.

[17] D. M. Carter, *States of Grace: Senegalese in Italy and the New Europe Immigration* (Minneapolis: University of Minnesota Press, 1997). For other studies of Murid migration, see Victoria Ebin, "International Networks of Trading Diaspora: The Mourides of Senegal Abroad," in *La ville à guichets fermés: Itinéraires, réseaux et insertion urbaine,* ed. Philippe Antoine and Abdoulaye Bara Diop (Paris: ORSTOM, 1995), 323–36; Scott L. Malcomson, "West of Eden: The Mouride Ethic and the Spirit of Capitalism," *Transition* 71 (1996): 24–43; Mamadou Diouf, "The Senegalese Murid Trade Diaspora and the Making

in Touba—making of it an international city, a cosmopolitan gathering place.

The Baraka of Gathering

Once in Touba, the itinerary of pilgrims includes *ziyāra* or visitations of the holy sites, the most important of which are the Grand Mosque and the tomb of Ahmadu Bamba. Lines are seemingly endless, and pilgrims wait hours in the hot sun for a few moments of physical nearness to the locations said to store Bamba's *baraka.*[18] Many pilgrims, however, do not make it even once to the area of the Grand Mosque. Some journeyers to Touba rest exclusively in familial homes where they lodge with relatives and friends. This is particularly true of women who are in charge of cooking for guests and taking care of children. Those who travel to Touba in religious associations such as *daaras* and *dahiras* will often pass the days and nights in their host residences, satisfied with fellowship among themselves.[19] Choosing not to fight their way through the crowds, these pilgrims explain that Bamba never ordered the formation of massive lines around monuments built after his death on the day of the *magal*. Bamba's *baraka* is not transmitted through such perfunctory itineraries of pilgrimage. Rather, what is essential is the act of placing one's feet within the borders of Touba, whether near to or far from the mausoleum of the shaykh.

---

of a Vernacular Cosmopolitanism," trans. Steven Rendall, *Public Culture* 12, no. 3 (2000): 679–702.

[18] According to Christian Coulon, in West African traditions, the saints of Sufi orders are believed to be sources of *baraka* that can be imparted to the community of believers even after their deaths. These traditions thus encourage journeys into sacred spaces as a means of gaining *baraka.* Coulon suggests that this belief in the transferability of *baraka* is one reason for the *magal*'s popularity within the Muridiyya. Coulon, "The Grand Magal in Touba," 195–210.

[19] The *daara* ("school") is a religious society that develops disciples spiritually through education and work. Formerly, *daara* designated a rural agricultural community serving one marabout. The *dahira* ("circle," "association") began as a mutual aid organization providing disciples in urban areas with opportunities for religious instruction, fellowship, and networking. Today, *dahiras* are numerous, and can be rural and urban, local, regional, and transnational, and can take on diverse functions and goals in addition to their traditional roles. For the history of Murid *dahiras,* see Momar Coumba Diop, "Fonctions et activités de dahira mourides urbains (Sénégal)," *Cahiers d'Études Africaines* 21, nos. 81–83 (1982): 79–91; Cheikh Anta Babou, "Brotherhood Solidarity, Education and Migration: The Role of the *Dahiras* Among the Murid Muslim Community of New York," *African Affairs* 403 (2002): 151–70; and Sophie Bava, "Le dahira urbain: Lieu de pouvoir du mouridisme," *Les Annales de la Recherche Urbaine* 96 (2004): 135–43.

What is critical is that one spends the 18th of Safar upon the blessed soil of the city, with other believers in grateful, communal remembrance. Following the interpretation of these participants, the *magal* of Touba is not primarily an occasion for obligatory *ziyāra* to static monuments, for the mechanical transfer of *baraka.* Rather, it is a time of gathering, and it is the experience of gathering—of physical and spiritual closeness to other believers—that imparts to the sacred journey its loftiness and profundity.

This ability of the pilgrimage to gather bodies and hearts in gratitude is one reason why Serigne Atou Diagne of Hizbut-Tarqiyyah calls Touba "a city of great rush."[20]

> It is what the experts in human geography, demographers, and town planners call "a pilgrimage city." But to avoid misunderstanding that can lead us to be qualified of fanatic, reformist, or associator, we stick to the statute of a "town of great rush," the flows of which must be controlled. This function is related to the status of a holy place of the city where believers go to at a precise moment of the year (18th of the lunar month of Safar) to express gratitude towards God for his immeasurable benefits, to dedicate an exclusive worship to him through laudable practices, invocations to obtain the favors of God, and intense activities to vivify and revive the fervent faith of a slave of God to the exclusive glory of his Lord.[21]

According to the scholars of Hizbut-Tarqiyyah, believers rush to Touba on the 18th of Safar for collective worship, to participate in intensely social expressions of faith on a grand scale. Rejecting characterizations of West African Sufi pilgrimages as festivities in which followers aim for passive reception of *baraka,*[22] Hizbut-Tarqiyyah asserts that crowds flow

---

[20] Hizbut-Tarqiyyah (*ḥizb al-tarqīya*) signifies "faction of (spiritual) elevation." The organization was born as the Dahira of Murid Students in 1975. From the beginning, the Dahira of Murid Students sought to promote the cultural values of Muridism by encouraging Arabic literacy and study of Bamba's works, among other things. Recognizing their impact, Caliph-General Serigne Saliou Mbacké promoted the organization to Daara Hizbut-Tarqiyyah in 1992. Since then, the organization has expanded its activities and projects, which include the creation of l'Institut International d'Études et de Recherche sur le Mouridisme (IIERM; International Institute for Studies and Research on Muridism). Hizbut-Tarqiyyah is particularly renowned for their wonderful performances of Bamba's poems. See Guèye, *Touba,* 239–47.

[21] Serigne Atou Diagne, *The Holy City of Touba: A Religious City of Multiple Functions,* pamphlet of the Grand Exhibition on Muridism (Touba: IIERM, Hizbut-Tarqiyyah, 2012).

[22] Hizbut-Tarqiyyah's position contrasts with that of previous scholars who have questioned the spiritual rigor of the *magal*. For example, Cruise O'Brien described the event as "a spec-

to Touba for the sake of sociable spiritual action: to imitate, together, the devotion and thanksgiving of Bamba, God's fervent slave.

Bamba's instructions for the *magal* were straightforward: "On this day, each person, wherever he may be, is called upon to consecrate all that he is able and to sacrifice offerings from camel to chicken; each, individually, is called upon to dispose of the offerings which are within his means."[23] Some believers maintain that Bamba also recommended the reading of the Qur'an and the singing of his poetry, and that he approved of expenditures fathers made on clothes and gifts for their families. Qur'anic recitation and sung poetry, the pleasure of new fabrics, animal sacrifices as small as a chicken and according to one's resources— the felicity that these simple tasks can engender suggests that Bamba envisioned his *magal* as a ritual means for believers to dwell in the joy of faith as it is lived in the world.

The contemporary celebration of the *magal* captures the spirit of sociability, gratitude, and joy that Bamba's original instructions intended. During the magal, the *daaras, dahiras,* and residents of Touba take it upon themselves to lodge and feed the millions of believers who travel to the city. Individuals and organizations rival each other in generosity, and enormous quantities of tasty drinks, delectable plates, fruits, sweets, and spicy black coffee are freely given to visitors. Hizbut-Tarqiyyah disposed of 16,000 chickens during the Grand Magal of 2012, while the popular leader Cheikh Béthio Thioune provided his followers with more than 1,000 cows.[24]

> Food is prepared and given to everybody, without distinction, without discrimination—neither of race, nor of religion . . . nor with regard to socio-professional categories, whether you are a factory worker or a butcher . . . to celebrate the Magal, Cheikh Béthio has, with his disciples, paid for 1000 cows, and camels, and sheep, and thousands and thousands of chickens. One cannot even count the number of the animals he has de-

---

tacle, an occasion for dispersed families to meet, and a country fair . . . The Khalifa-General is materially enriched by the donations of the Mourides during the Magal, a large proportion of which go to him" (*Mourides of Senegal,* 138). Similarly, Coulon maintained, "This pilgrimage has nothing to do with the esoteric aspect of Sufism, which is, incidentally, not highly developed in the Mouride brotherhood" ("The Grand Magal of Touba," 196).

[23] Sermon of Caliph-General Serigne Abdoul Ahad Mbacké before the Grand Magal of 1979, debut of Safar 1399H, Touba.

[24] Papa Assane Diouf (IIERM, Hizbut-Tarqiyyah), interview with author, Dakar, January 4, 2012; Moustapha Sall, interview with author, Touba, January 12, 2012.

> ployed for the needs of the Magal . . . That's the real spiritual work. He has done it with his followers. They do it with love, without any other intention, without hesitation. It's automatic. It's unconditional. (Amadou Moustapha Sall, leader of Daara Sant Serigne Saliou Wakeur Cheikh Béthio Touba-Colobane, interview with author, Touba, January 12, 2012)

In describing the blessedness of the *magal* experience, most pilgrims do not speak of *baraka* transmitted from the remains of the shaykh. Rather, they speak of the story of exile, the collective action of thanksgiving, the grandeur of gathering together. They speak of the gratuity of good food and drink, the copiousness of flesh sacrificed in Bamba's honor. They speak also of poetry, the copiousness of voices singing Bamba's *qaṣāʾid.*

Sufi Verses

During the *magal,* Touba pulsates with the voices of believers reciting *qaṣāʾid,* or poems. As crowds of millions descend upon the road leading to Touba, the sounds of *qaṣāʾid* emanate from almost all stereo speakers of vehicles on their way. Voices raised in singing *qaṣāʾid* constitute the sacred soundtrack of the pilgrim's journey and the blessed soundscape of the pilgrim's destination. Around the mosque, massive speakers continuously radiate recordings of Bamba's poems at extremely high volumes. Throughout the city, individuals and groups perform *qaṣāʾid* on corners and in streets, in courtyards and the residences of marabouts. The singing of *qaṣāʾid* is further heard in the concerts that electrify the different neighborhoods all night long. Complementing this primary sonic layer of poetry are the religious speeches and television broadcasts from other speakers, and the chatter and footsteps of pilgrims tightly packed in the downtown area. The acoustic aesthetic is one of uncompromising saturation, as if to silence any possible question within the listener as to where she might be. During the *magal,* sounds announce more persistently than any other medium that one has arrived in Touba.

For many, the soundtrack of *magal* facilitates a state of meditation. "The *qaṣāʾid* help me concentrate on the shaykh and God and the purpose of the *magal.*"[25] Pilgrims enjoy listening to the singing of *qaṣāʾid* in silence, or humming along or reciting softly, walking to their rhythms

[25] Khabane Wade, interview with author, Touba, January 10, 2012.

while fighting their way through the crowds. Outside, in the midst of the crowds and the chaos, copies of *qaṣāʾid* are sold by ambulant vendors, and pilgrims read multicolored editions of the poems while waiting to visit the sacred sites.

Pilgrims consistently describe the sonic environment as *neex*—good, sweet, agreeable. *Neex* is used to describe delicious food, alluring scents, attractive women, agreeable experiences, beautiful voices. *Neex* implies physical pleasure, what satisfies the individual on a sensual level. While Bamba's *qaṣāʾid* carry sacred messages, the addition of the beautiful voice evokes the sensation of *neex,* of sweetness and of delight.

In these *qaṣāʾid* (*qaṣīda,* singular), Bamba gave to his followers a distinct, unique liturgy that would be completely their own—that would textually and acoustically differentiate their worship from those of other Muslims in the region and in the larger *umma* of believers. Originally, the term *qaṣīda* referred to a variety of pre-Islamic Arabic poetry sustaining a uniform meter and a single end rhyme throughout.[26] Though Bamba did not obey this classical form, the term *qaṣāʾid* is applied to his works, as it is often to Arabic poems in general. In Senegal, the term *qaṣāʾid* is foremost associated with Bamba's poetry. The Wolofized version of the word, *xasaayid,* is well entrenched in vernacular speech and evokes the Murid founder. Arabist Khadim Mbacké explains, "Ahmadu Bamba essentially wrote in the Arabic language . . . I haven't seen a single writing in another language. He wrote only in Arabic. Additionally, he privileged poetry over prose. One even has the impression that he was more comfortable when he wrote poetry than when he wrote prose."[27]

According to Murid tradition, Bamba's writings in totality weighed more than seven tons. While about seventy *qaṣāʾid* are in general circulation, the exact number of poems that Bamba wrote cannot be confirmed.[28]

---

[26] Stefan Sperl and Christopher Shackle, eds., *Qasida Poetry in Islamic Asia and Africa,* 2 vols. (Leiden: E. J. Brill, 1996).

[27] Khadim Mbacké (Institut Fondamental d'Afrique Noire [IFAN], University of Cheikh Anta Diop), interview with author, Dakar, October 12, 2012. As a descendant of Bamba born in Touba, Khadim Mbacké can claim a more than ordinary experience of and access to the shaykh's writings.

[28] In 1985, Abdou Malal Diop confirmed 49 poems attributable to Bamba. Since then, more poems have become available. Currently, compilations sold by independent vendors can include close to seventy poems attributable to Bamba. Abdoul Malal Diop, "Traduction et commentaire du Viatique des Jeunes d'Ahmadou Bamba," Third-cycle doctoral thesis, University of Dakar, 1985, appendices.

Most Murids believe that innumerable poems of the shaykh are yet to be revealed, as they were hidden or destroyed.[29] Submerged in the sea, tossed down wells, buried in secret locations, most of his works are said to be presently concealed, protected from eyes not meant to grasp them.

Bamba's poems were written in a fluid, profuse Arabic that is, however, strikingly particular. Khadim Mbacké confirms: "Ahmadu Bamba mastered Arabic. But sometimes when he wrote in Arabic, especially with the poems, he took many liberties. Perhaps it was the Sufism, because in general, what interested Sufis were not the rules created by scientists. What interested them was expressing well what they wanted. Bamba's Arabic was an idiosyncratic Arabic unlike any other. Perhaps one could call it *esoteric*."[30] In Bamba's unique style, one sees evidence of the profound mysticism that preoccupied him, and perhaps, caused him to disregard the conventional rules of grammar and syntax. This immersion in Sufi mysticism resulted, nevertheless, in beautiful, albeit noncompliant and esoteric verse. While lauded for his contributions to Senegalese and Sufi literature,[31] Bamba was not primarily concerned with the beauty of language as such. Khadim Mbacké elaborates: "What interested the author was not the literary quality of the poems, but, above all, the content of the poems—the act of truly thanking God, and of stirring others to thank God by writing texts easy to memorize, easy to recite. He was not fastidious in choosing the words, in conforming strictly to the rules established by the 'profane,' the '*exoteric.*'"

In their themes, as in their style, Bamba's *qaṣāʾid* reveal their character as Sufi expressions of grace. The *qaṣāʾid* invariably communicate ardent love for God and unwavering faith in his will. Many of the poems are odes to the Prophet Mohamed and his companions. Others discuss the oneness of Allah, the five pillars of Islam, and the obligations of a Muslim life. In some verses, Bamba implores divine intervention in the battles raging within and without the soul. He prays for assistance against the oppression that he and his followers endured at the hands of the colonialists; he prays likewise for aid in transcending the vanities of his own ego, vanities

[29] I have not met one person willing to give a ballpark estimate of the number of poems Bamba wrote.

[30] Khadim Mbacké, interview with author, Dakar, October 12, 2012.

[31] See Amar Samb, *Essai sur la contribution du Sénégal à la literature d'expression arabe* (Dakar: IFAN, 1972); and Fernand Dumont, *La pensée religieuse d'Amadou Bamba* (Dakar: Nouvelles editions africaines, 1975).

preventing union with the ultimate, heavenly source. All of the poems are consistently passionate, bursting with intense longing to return to the presence of God.

Musical Legitimacy

Bamba's *qaṣāʾid* are sung, and this singing is as distinctive as it is pervasive. However, *qaṣāʾid* are not songs. Singing provides the context for *qaṣīda* performance—for the public manifestation and communal experience of the verses. Singing does not, strictly speaking, transform these Islamic devotional texts into songs. Papa Assane Diouf of Hizbut-Tarqiyyah states, "To sing the *qaṣāʾid* and to sing—these are not equivalent. When one sings and dances, it is not the *qaṣāʾid* that one sings. Songs are invented with the modes with which they are sung. A *qaṣīda* is a poem written by Shaykh Ahmadu Bamba that one sings."[32] Along these lines, the singing of *qaṣāʾid* should be vigilantly disassociated with music—with instruments, dance, and the profane sentiments aroused by too much sonic stimulation. While enjoying a melodiously opulent recording of a *qaṣīda,* Khabane Wade asserts, "This is not music. Music has other components, guitars and such. It resembles music, but it has nothing to do with music."[33]

The relationship between *qaṣāʾid,* singing, and music sparks a heated and ongoing debate within the Muridiyya. For many, Bamba's *qaṣāʾid* should be approached with the same conscientiousness and ritual cleanliness demanded for the Qur'an. Thus, one should not touch, recite, or sing the poems until the required ablutions have been completed. Above all, one should not deform the *qaṣāʾid* by introducing questionable musical practices. Murid preachers often warn against an excess of melodic and rhythmic excitement in *qaṣīda* performance. In 2011, a group of young Murid professionals formed the movement *1111 murid contre l'usage des xassida à des fin musicales* ("1111 Murids against the use of *qaṣāʾid* for musical purposes"). In their crusade against the musical performance of Bamba's poems, *1111 murid* is endorsed by several Murid leaders and organizations, and counts more than 1,500 supporters on Facebook.

These vehement denunciations of music are directed, in particular, at a widespread phenomenon in Senegal: the exploitation of sacred texts in

[32] Papa Assane Diouf (IIERM, Hizbut-Tarqiyyah), interview with author, Dakar, May 12, 2012.

[33] Khabane Wade, interview with author, Touba, January 10, 2012.

popular music of all genres.[34] Indeed, it is difficult to name a Senegalese popular musician who has not incorporated Bamba's poems or other local religious texts in her compositions and concerts. That Bamba's sacred verses should be recklessly belched while accompanied by electric guitars and frenetic drums, in the midst of erotic dancing in nightclubs, is a source of indignation for many. Preacher Serigne Saliou Sow protests, "These poems are based on Qur'anic texts. And it's deplorable that the Qur'an should be sung in milieus where men and women rub against each other or where there is drinking of prohibited beverages. Such practices show disrespect toward God and his prophet."[35] However, popular musicians are not the only Murids who combine *qaṣāʾid* with musical practices. In a number of Murid milieus, during gatherings for celebration and fellowship, Bamba's poems are sung while accompanied by drums and dance. Moreover, some individuals do not hesitate to designate Bamba's *qaṣāʾid* the "music of the Muridiyya."

Naturally, the debate on *qaṣīda* performance reflects the centuries-old polemic pursued by Muslim jurists, Sufi philosophers, and other thinkers on the legality of music and the permissibility of musical recitation of the Qur'an.[36] While Murid opinions on the legitimacy of music vary, the musical recitation of Bamba's *qaṣāʾid* is broadly, almost unanimously accepted. Passing over the semantics of the debate, most Murids with whom I have spoken are not unwilling to consider the musical recitation of Bamba's poems a form of singing. In *qaṣīda* performance, what is controversial is music, understood here as involving instruments, irreverent settings, and

---

[34] The profusion of Islamic topics and texts in West African popular music is a phenomenon that has been noted by several scholars, and merits much more comprehensive study. Fiona McLaughlin's two articles provide a good introduction to the subject of Islam and popular music in the Senegalese context. See Fiona McLaughlin, "Islam and Popular Music in Senegal: The Emergence of a 'New Tradition,'" *Africa* 67, no. 4 (1997): 560–81; "'In the Name of God I Will Sing Again, Mawdo Malick the Good': Popular Music and Senegalese Sufi Tariqas," *Journal of Religion in Africa* 30, no. 2 (2000): 191–207; Eric Charry, *Mande Music: Traditional and Modern Music of the Maninka and Mandinka of Western Africa* (Chicago: University of Chicago Press, 2000), 22; Patricia Tang, *Masters of the Sabar: Wolof Griot Percussionists of Senegal* (Philadelphia: Temple University Press, 2007), 155.

[35] Serigne Saliou Sow, interview with *1111 murid,* https://www.facebook.com/video/video.php?v=1928288719719.

[36] Kristina Nelson's landmark study on Qur'anic recitation contains one of the most balanced and well-documented analyses of the debate on listening to music and musical recitation. See Kristina Nelson, *The Art of Reciting the Qur'an* (New York: University in Cairo Press, 2001), 32–51.

inappropriate behavior. Unaccompanied singing, however, is not controversial—as long as that singing avoids the excess of musicality that detracts from spirituality:

> With this music and with those instruments, eventually it is no longer the content that is important. It is the sound. Musicality is above. Yet, it should be the contrary. When you listen to what we sing, however beautiful the sound, it is always the message that is above. However, when I take my guitar and those instruments, I can no longer emphasize what he wrote and what he expressed. Rather it is the sounds that end up dominating the content. When you sing the *qaṣāʾid,* you should leave this base world of easy carnal pleasure. It should be a moment to travel spiritually. This can only happen with a purely religious concentration as if one is in prayer. (Papa Assane Diouf, International Institute for Studies and Research on Muridism, Hizbut-Tarqiyyah, interview with author, Dakar, May 12, 2012)

Legitimately, the *qaṣāʾid* can be read (the French *lire*), recited (*réciter*), and sung (*chanter*). In conversing in French, the majority use the term "singing" to refer to recordings and live performances of *qaṣāʾid* ("chanter les *qaṣāʾid*"). Indeed, the rich melodization and robust vocality of *qaṣīda* performance justifies, musicologically speaking, use of the term "singing." In this context, recitation more often refers to the repetition of lines of the poems in a less melodious or less continuous manner—as in sermons and speeches. Recitation is also the privileged mode of those who claim to have unpleasant voices; these disciples never sing the *qaṣāʾid,* but do read them silently and recite them aloud when the occasion requires.

The terms for the practice of *qaṣāʾid* are more illuminating in Wolof than they are in French or English. The Wolofization of the word—*xasaayid*—is more often heard in Senegal than the Arabic pronunciation. Bamba's *xasaayid* are associated with two verbs: *woy,* to sing; and *jang,* to learn, study, or read. *Jang* has also come to mean to recite or sing a religious text. *Jang xasaayid* can be used interchangeably with *woy xasaayid* to designate the singing of Bamba's poems. The synonymy of the two terms in Wolof—*jang* and *woy,* reading and singing—suggests this possibility: in the practice of sacred poetry, singing can be synonymous with reading. Singing can be a form of studying, a form of learning, a form of knowing.

The ultimate reference for Murid positions on *qaṣāʾid* performance is Bamba himself. By all accounts, he delighted in the singing of his poems. "He loved listening to people sing his *qaṣāʾid,*" confirms Khadim Mbacké.[37] The public, communal singing of the poems was a common occurrence during Bamba's stay in colonial Diourbel, between 1912 and 1927. Research by Hizbut-Tarqiyyah's International Institute for Studies and Research on Muridism suggests that the singing of *qaṣāʾid* was ordered, guided, and perhaps initiated by Bamba himself.[38] According to Papa Assane Diouf,

> He had a group of twelve people who correctly mastered the *qaṣāʾid.* They read and sang them correctly . . . each time that the shaykh wrote a *qaṣīda,* when they were there, he gave it to them, and they sang it . . . and that's the source from which we have taken the melodies that you hear now. We have not invented new melodies. We refer to the melodies of the elders . . . sometimes it was he himself who took the *qaṣāʾid* and sang them aloud. In listening, his disciples imitated him in that work. There is a heritage, and it is inherited, and it has been passed down to us. (Papa Assane Diouf, International Institute for Studies and Research on Muridism, Hizbut-Tarqiyyah, interview with author, Dakar, May 12, 2012)

According to this research, Bamba was not only a poet. He was also a singer of his own poems.[39]

Sufi Voices

Since Bamba's time, the *qaṣāʾid* have been sung collectively and individually. Collectively, disciples congregate in groups called *kureels,* which literally means committee or organization. *Kureels* vary in number, and can contain from as few as three to more than thirty members. The members of a single *kureel* usually belong to the same *dahira* or *daara,*[40] or have sworn allegiance to the same religious leader. The vocal agility and Arabic

[37] Khadim Mbacké, interview with author, Dakar, October 12, 2012.

[38] Hizbut-Tarqiyyah has been conducting inquiries into *qaṣāʾid* performance for more than thirty years.

[39] That Bamba occasionally sang his *qaṣāʾid* is a possibility that has not been unanimously confirmed. However, it is a position that has been expressed often in my conversations with performers of *qaṣāʾid.*

[40] For definitions of the religious associations *dahira* and *daara,* see note 19.

literacy of *kureels* can vary dramatically. The *kureels* of Hizbut-Tarqiyyah expect a high degree of Arabic competence, and train members in vocal control and choral unity. Their dependably masterful performances are widely considered paradigms for *kureel* singing.[41] Some *kureels* perform from memory, championing the ingraining of the sacred verses "in the mind" and "in the heart."[42] Other *kureels* habitually guard the texts—often beautifully bound—before them, in the middle of the singing circle. The presence of the words directly in front of them reminds singers to concentrate on the message, to avoid being carried away by flights of musical fancy. In collective performance, what *is* customary is that *kureel* members stand or sit in a circle, as the first singers of *qaṣāʾid* did before Bamba.

Almost all *kureel* members with whom I have spoken trace their performance lineage back to Bamba himself. *Kureels* typically assert that they inherited their tradition of singing from an elder or leader directly connected to Bamba. These elders are said to have invented the melodies, rhythms, and vocal stylings with which the poems are now sung. The elders sang before Bamba, and he approved their inventions. Some claim that the shaykh was even directly involved in the creation of melodies. Where it is acknowledged that a melody is an invention of a living disciple, one legitimizes it by arguing that it follows the spirit of melodies loved by the shaykh. The musical choices made in *qaṣīda* performance are thus justified by appealing to religious lineage and spiritual authenticity, by professing an "ethics of style."[43]

When sung individually, *qaṣāʾid* can gain melodies, rhythms, elaborations, and improvisations that are awkward in the *kureel* setting.[44] Prominent soloists of *qaṣāʾid* usually possess brilliant technique and puissant, sublime voices. Often, these gifted soloists trace their lineage back to the

---

[41] For an excellent example of *kureel* singing, see Hizbut-Tarqiyyah, *Midādī,* Gamou of 2011, Touba, http://www.youtube.com/watch?v=0RhydS_6Sx0. *Midādī* is a poem that Bamba wrote during his exile in Mauritania from 1903 to 1907.

[42] Amadou Moustapha Sall, interview with the author, Touba, January 12, 2012.

[43] The "ethics of style" is a model developed by Timothy Rommen to address the pivotal role of ethics in decisions on musical style. See Timothy Rommen, *Mek Some Noise: Gospel Music and the Ethics of Style in Trinidad* (Berkeley: University of California Press, 2007).

[44] For a solo performance featuring a beautiful voice, see Serigne Ibra Gueye, *Rumnā shukūr,* http://www.youtube.com/watch?v=Er9Oy60Pups. *Rumnā shukūr* is a poem that Bamba wrote during his Gabon exile, 1895–1902.

griot caste of musicians.[45] Performances can be extremely passionate, the voice expertly communicating the gamut of feeling from spiritual ecstasy to spiritual despair. Most often, celebrated soloists sing melodies that they have composed themselves, without appealing to the authority of an ancient disciple or religious leader. However, that the melodies be "respectful" of Bamba's verses, and that one can imagine Bamba delighting in them, is still a standard for judging the religious authenticity of solo performances.

Whether singing collectively or individually, the voice of *qaṣāʾid* should be agreeable, and it should be trained in Arabic pronunciation and Islamic psalmody.[46] The voice of *qaṣāʾid* is also unique, localized, and innovative. While building upon pan-Islamic rules for the vocalization of religious Arabic poetry, *qaṣīda* performance also draws from trans-regional styles of devotional singing that can be heard in Sufi communities in Morocco, Iran, and South Asia.[47] In addition to the musical heritage of Islam and Sufism, the third foundation of the voice of *qaṣāʾid* performance is the indigenous praise singing of griots, hereditary caste musicians in West Africa.[48] These multiple geographic and cultural roots are fused in the vocal tradition prized in *qaṣīda* performance.

---

[45] Thomas Hale, "Islam and the Griots in West Africa: Bridging the Gap Between Traditions," *Africana Journal* 13 (1982): 84–90; Fiona McLaughlin, "Islam and Popular Music in Senegal: The Emergence of a 'New Tradition,'" *Africa* 67, no. 4 (1997): 560–81.

[46] I speak here of the "ideal" voice, and describe qualities I notice in the remarkable, celebrated singers of *qaṣāʾid.* With the proliferation of *kureels* and the democratization of singing, one often comes across performances that diverge significantly from what is described here. However, there is a respected tradition of *qaṣīda* singing, and most performers model themselves after this tradition, which is briefly introduced here.

[47] Islamic religious singing is called *al-inshād al-dīnī,* and is described in Nelson, *The Art of Reciting the Qur'an;* and Michael Frishkopf, "Tarab in the Mystic Sufi Chant of Egypt," in *Colors of Enchantment: Visual and Performing Arts of the Middle East,* ed. Sherifa Zuhur (Cairo: American University in Cairo Press, 2001). For the vocal aesthetics of Sufi music, see Regula Qureshi, *Sufi Music of India and Pakistan: Sound, Context, and Meaning in Qawwali* (Chicago: University of Chicago Press, 1997); and A. J. Racy, *Making Music in the Arab World: The Culture and Artistry of Tarab* (Oxford: Oxford University Press, 2002).

[48] Ruth M. Stone, *Dried Millet Breaking: Time, Words, and Songs in the Wòi Epic of the Kpelle* (Bloomington: Indiana University Press, 1988); Laura Arnston Harris, "The Play of Ambiguity in Praise-Song Performance: A Definition of the Genre Through an Examination of Its Practice in Northern Sierra Leone" (Ph.D. dissertation, Indiana University, 1992); Thomas A. Hale, *Griots and Griottes: Masters of Words and Music* (Bloomington: Indiana University Press, 1998).

The voice of *qaṣāʾid* is an unusually piercing voice; a wide voice—with a range of nearly two octaves, able to soar and to descend; a broad voice—of exceptional timbral flexibility, capable of conjuring a diverse palette of tonal colors. The singing is expressive and improvisatory, relying on modally inflected melodies, intricate ornamentation, cycles of tension and release, shifts in register and dynamics, and selective use of nasality, hoarseness, and reinforced falsetto—all markers of Sufi and Islamic influence. In addition to this musical heritage of Islam and Sufism, the voice in *qaṣāʾid* is often heroic in style, tense in quality, and forceful in delivery—from the top of the lungs declaiming strongly pulsed, quasi-metrical, lengthy phrases, dwelling at the highest register possible without transition into head voice—all traits of indigenous griot praise singing.[49]

The voice of *qaṣāʾid* is also, categorically, a male voice. While performances by female soloists and female *kureels* have become more apparent in recent years, they are still the highly controversial exception and not the rule. Customarily, women sit apart from men who sing *qaṣāʾid.* They listen, silently. Young girls can learn to chant the poems aloud in *daaras* or Qur'anic schools. However, once adult, they are generally discouraged from doing so publicly, in mixed company. A woman can, however, sing *qaṣāʾid* before her husband, as "all things are permitted before one's husband." The reason often offered for the inadvisability of female public performance is the excessive beauty of a mature woman's voice. Singing, ideally, should fortify the religious message and deepen spirituality. The sensual exquisiteness of a woman's voice, on the other hand, could distract men from spiritual concentration. It can bind Bamba's verses to pleasures of the carnal world.

Sung Journeys

Bamba once said, "The *qaṣāʾid* are like birds: those who sing them are like the wings; those who listen, like the feathers."[50] In this image, it is singing that gives wings to sacred poetry, that allows it to fly. Like feathers, listening is also essential to the flight of poetry. In this way, those who only lis-

[49] The aspects of the voice described here are most striking in the singing of famous soloists.

[50] Recounted by Caliph-General Serigne Saliou Mbacké in a meeting with Daara Hizbut-Tarqiyyah, Touba, October 18, 1997.

ten—whether because of vocal inadequacy or gender conventions—also actively participate in the community of singing that has formed around the *qaṣāʾid.* As several advocates of listening have reminded me, "A bird cannot fly without its feathers."

In the contemporary moment, singing continues to translate Bamba's esoteric Arabic poetry into accessible, communal, and communicable practice, as it had done in the early years of the Muridiyya. In Senegal's cities, Bamba's *qaṣāʾid* are heard constantly in taxis and buses, in stores and homes. *Kureels* assemble in private and in public—very frequently, very audibly, unapologetically singing throughout the night. Ubiquitous fixtures of marketplaces, recordings of unaccompanied *qaṣāʾid* are generated and distributed with great speed. Sung *qaṣāʾid* rank, by some estimates, among the best-selling genres in Senegal. They are certainly the most audible, saturating the soundscape of commercial and national life.

The sounds of *qaṣāʾid* have also traveled far beyond the borders of the nation. Embedded in transnationalized recordings, performed by brilliant singers in concerts abroad, and sung by Senegalese immigrants—the sounds of *qaṣāʾid* materially demarcate the ever-expanding boundaries of the religious diaspora. The *dahiras* of the diaspora lay emphasis on the performance and teaching of *qaṣāʾid.* Thus, many Murids who did not study Arabic in Senegal learn to read Bamba's poems while frequenting *dahira* meetings abroad. This diasporic devotion to sacred poetry is especially evident in the new trend of Qaṣīda Day. Public celebrations dedicated to Bamba's poetry, Qaṣīda Days are organized by *dahiras* in Italy, Canada, and the United States. They bring *kureels* and soloists from across the globe to Milan, Montreal, Detroit, New York, and, in the future, Philadelphia[51]—making these cities new centers of *qaṣīda* singing. For Papa Assane Diouf, Qaṣīda Day is an effective way for diasporic Murids to reconnect to the spiritual home. "Through *qaṣāʾid* they express their link to Touba."[52]

Indeed, *qaṣāʾid* are portable reminders of religious roots, and diasporic Murids speak of them with emotion and gratitude. "In listening, as in reading, my soul is delighted. What I feel when I listen to *qaṣāʾid,* I cannot describe it, no one can describe it."[53] The reading of the poems are, for some, as effective as direct supplication to God. "If I have a hardship, [they] are my source of healing . . . if I want something, I might wake up

---

[51] Mbacké Thioune, interview with author, Philadelphia, November 4, 2010.

[52] Pape Assane Diouf, interview with author, Dakar, January 4, 2012.

[53] Khabane Wade, interview with author, Touba, January 10, 2012.

in the middle of the night and pray and read the *qaṣāʾid.* Most of the time my prayers are answered."[54] Some believe that Bamba's verses can provide healing, protection, and good fortune. "If you are sick, and you read them in the morning or in the afternoon . . . I have had the experience of reading them while sick, and being healed."[55] Murids speak of the *baraka* of Bamba's verses, a *baraka* that can be transferred through reading or vocalization. "The recitation of *qaṣāʾid* will bring *baraka* to you, and will relax you, and will make you loved by people."[56] Communion with Bamba's words can reunite believers viscerally with their beloved saint. "When I read the *qaṣāʾid,* it's like I'm face to face with Ahmadu Bamba."[57] *Qaṣāʾid* can substitute for the traditional Sufi guides that help the believer approach God. "If you want to go to God, if you want to be with God, even if you don't have a spiritual guide, you can get there with the *qaṣāʾid.*"[58] Some even believe that the *qaṣāʾid* pave a straight path toward salvation. "Just by reading it, even if someone is not a Muslim, he is not going to go to hell. He is going to paradise."[59]

For many, the sonorities of the words divulge their mystic meanings. "You got some deep things inside the *qaṣāʾid* that people don't know . . . it comes through the sound."[60] In this view, it is not the existence of *qaṣāʾid* on the page that delivers the spiritual message; rather, it is the audition of the words—their utterance by the voice and their absorption through the ears—that leads to illumination. "When you sing the *qaṣāʾid,* there is a spiritual light that you can receive."[61] Even if one does not grasp Bamba's *qaṣāʾid* grammatically or semantically, "when you sing it, sometimes you may understand the words that were written."[62]

In describing the personal experience of singing, believers commonly state that they feel happiness, they feel high, they feel as if they are in another world. "When I sing with my friends, my core disciples, when we stand up and I sing, I feel high."[63] They are "transported" by commu-

[54] Mbacké Thioune, interview with author, Philadelphia, November 4, 2010.
[55] Khabane Wade, interview with author, Touba, January 10, 2012.
[56] Mbacké Thioune, interview with author, Philadelphia, November 4, 2010.
[57] Badou Mbengue, interview with author, Philadelphia, October 31, 2010.
[58] Dame Diene, interview with author, Philadelphia, November 4, 2010.
[59] Badou Mbengue, interview with author, Philadelphia, October 31, 2010.
[60] Badou Mbengue, interview with author, Philadelphia, October 31, 2010.
[61] Dame Diene, interview with author, Philadelphia, November 4, 2010.
[62] Dame Diene, interview with author, Philadelphia, November 4, 2010.
[63] Dame Diene, interview with author, Philadelphia, November 4, 2010.

nal, unaccompanied singing into transcendent realms where there is no distance between themselves, their beloved Bamba, and God.[64] Singing can even transport believers to places of profound emotion where pure felicity causes "crying, dying . . . it is only *qaṣāʾid* that makes us feel that."[65] Along with sensations of blissful death, many performers of *qaṣāʾid* reach ecstasy—manifested through trancelike behaviors such as throwing their heads against walls and cutting themselves with knives—without incurring bodily harm.[66]

The act of singing, especially when accomplished in groups, is often spoken of as a journey away from the carnal world. It is a sonic journey that elevates, that liberates, that takes one to an intangible space higher and farther. In addition to revealing visions of paradise beyond, the singing of *qaṣāʾid* can also transport Murids to paradise on earth, to the blessed abode of Touba. "You can stay here singing and shutting your eyes and [feel like] being in Touba—entering the mosque, entering the cemetery, entering the places and houses of the shaykh."[67] Especially when shared within a group, the singing of *qaṣāʾid* collapses the distance between one's diasporic position and one's spiritual origin. "Even though we are too far from Touba, when we do this here, it takes us to Touba, because of what you can imagine, *oh man*! It reminds me of when I was in the mosque, in Ahmadu Bamba's mausoleum . . . it's another world."[68]

Listening intently, listening deeply to sung poetry can also transport a believer. "When *really* listening to *qaṣāʾid,* it is like you are in Touba."[69] While listening to the singing of Bamba's verses, one can feel "as if in paradise. I feel as if I am in Touba."[70] Here, we are reminded of Serigne Saliou Mbacké's metaphor: the *qaṣāʾid* are birds, the singers their wings, the lis-

---

[64] For an interesting study of how communal, unaccompanied singing can "transport" performers, see Caroline Bithell, *Transported by Song: Corsican Voices from Oral Tradition to World Stage* (Lanham, Md.: Scarecrow, 2007).

[65] Dame Diene, interview with author, Philadelphia, November 4, 2010.

[66] While *qaṣīda* singing is not music, literature on Sufi music and other Islamic repertoires has addressed transcendent and ecstatic experiences similar to those recounted here. See Qureshi, *Sufi Music of India and Pakistan;* Racy, *Making Music in the Arab World;* and Deborah Kapchan, *Traveling Spirit Masters: Moroccan Gnawa Trance and Music in the Global Marketplace* (Middleton, Conn.: Wesleyan University Press, 2007).

[67] Dame Diene, interview with author, Philadelphia, November 4, 2010.

[68] Badou Mbengue, interview with author, Philadelphia, October 31, 2010.

[69] Khabane Wade, interview with author, Touba, January 10, 2012.

[70] Abdou Karim Mbengue, interview with author, Touba, January 9, 2012.

teners their feathers. The listeners are as indispensable to the *qaṣāʾid*'s transcendence as the singers. And singing and listening are both intrinsic parts of Bamba's poems.

Exile as Piety

Transporting listeners and singers to Touba, *qaṣīda* performance sonically places believers in the sites imbued with the saint's presence, in his Grand Mosque, in his mausoleum. Through listening and singing, they imaginatively accomplish the itinerary of pilgrimage; they see the shaykh. However, Murids in diaspora do not confuse virtual pilgrimage with actual physical presence in the holy city. "It's not the same. In Touba, you are in another world. In Touba, it looks like you are in heaven."[71] This insistence on the actuality of Touba is based on awareness of the intense fellowship that the city enables. "In Touba, there will be the crowd, and it is said in Islam that worshipping with a group of people is better than worshipping alone. The bigger the group is, the better the worship is. The feeling will never be the same."[72] In addition, diasporic performances cannot imitate the sheer volume of singing in Touba, the immense poetic volume that proves the strength and breadth of the spiritual community. "When I am over there [in Italy] during the period of the *magal*, my spirit rests entirely in Touba . . . here[in Touba] it is more exciting, more pleasurable, there is more to see, all of your family . . . and here, you hear the singing of *qaṣāʾid* —everywhere, and all the time, all the time, all the time."[73] This is part of the incomparable grandeur of gathering for the *magal* in Touba: the bliss of listening to *qaṣāʾid* at the greatest volume possible, in the midst of as many believers as possible.

On that snowdrift winter night that opened this paper, the seventy individuals in that Philadelphia motel banquet room could not reproduce the volume of millions singing to Bamba during his Grand Magal in Touba. Aware of their inability to return physically to the spiritual home, they gather during the Grand Magal to celebrate their participation in a different imaginary of sacred journey—a contemporary imaginary that is connected to both the historical contexts and the deeper religious meanings of the pilgrimage dedicated to Bamba. For the date of the Grand Magal does

[71] Khabane Wade, interview with author, Touba, January 10, 2012.

[72] Dame Diene, interview with author, Philadelphia, November 4, 2010.

[73] Khabane Wade, interview with author, Touba, January 10, 2012.

not coincide with Bamba's birth or death. Rather, it takes place on the anniversary of his deportation by French colonial authorities to Gabon. Unwaveringly faithful, Bamba utilized his exile and his suffering as means towards spiritual elevation. Cheikh Anta Babou comments, "Sufis consider suffering as one of the forms by which humans can become aware of and even get closer to their creator. It is a means by which God disables his friend's *nafs* (carnal soul), purifies his soul, and increases his baraka."[74]

According to Murid tradition, Bamba spent his years in Gabon in prayer, in meditation, and in writing. Bamba may have been particularly prolific during the period of exile—as a way of disciplining his thoughts and feelings, of ascending to a place of metaphysical contemplation away from the physical hardships.[75] The poetry he conceived during exile does not obsess over injustice, does not fixate on suffering, does not despair. Rather, in his exilic poems, Bamba expresses passionate gratitude. Bamba does demand divine assistance against those who wish to harm him. However, what he demands most frequently and most ardently is aid in overcoming the battles raging within his own soul. In the poem *Wa Laqad Karramnā Banī 'Ādama* (*We Have Honored the Children of Adam*), composed while in exile in Gabon, Bamba writes:[76] "Fulfill the prayers of my soul and erase from me every flaw, expunge from me every evil and establish in me all that is beautiful. Accept and accomplish the prayers that I formulated in Touba, Touba which I have built through your grace alone."[77] Thus immersed in solitary worship for seven years, Bamba is believed to have emerged from exile even more imbued with God's grace. Cheikh Anta Babou offers: "Bamba certainly believed that by the time he left Gabon, he had reached the highest level of spiritual purity and blessedness. He

---

[74] Babou, *Fighting the Greater Jihad,* 134.

[75] The popular consensus is that Bamba wrote profusely while in Gabon. I thank Khadim Mbacké for first suggesting to me that Bamba may have employed writing as a means of enduring solitude.

[76] I am indebted to Papa Assane Diouf of Hizbut-Tarqiyyah's International Institute for Studies and Research on Muridism for identifying the period of composition of the exilic poems mentioned in this paper: *Wa Laqad Karramnā Banī 'Ādama, Rumnā shukūr* (see note 44) and *Midādī* (see note 41 and the last page of this paper).

[77] Ahmadu Bamba Mbacké, *Wa Laqad Karramnā Banī 'Ādama* (Dakar: Imprimerie Serigne Issa Niang, n.d.), 7. For a recording in which the Arabic text is displayed, see *Wa Laqad Karramnā Banī 'Ādama,* Kurel Ahlul Minan, http://www.youtube.com/watch?v=-JdANKxL__0. For an audiovisual recording, see *Wa Laqad Karramnā Banī 'Ādama,* Hizbut-Tariyyah, Gamou 2012, http://www.youtube.com/watch?v=3Bcm4HU7pB4&feature=related.

openly made this claim in his writings. In *Jazaau Shakuur,* for example, he declared, 'It was while in the Island (Mayumba) that I was shown and cured of all my imperfections.' "[78]

In Murid hagiographies reconstructing exile—most notably, the epic Wolof poetry of Musa Ka—Bamba's spiritual journey acquires a linear, albeit beautiful narrative coherence that tends towards triumphalism. This narrative would set Bamba's return from exile as the date of victory against enemies, the date of the coronation of the hero, the obvious date of celebration. In Bamba's own writing, however, the enemy is not, ultimately, the French colonial authority; the enemy is, most essentially, one's own carnal soul. Thus, Bamba speaks of his "triumph" during exile as being "cured" of his imperfections, of the sickness within himself. The physical exile in which he crossed the sea into the heart of hostile lands to suffer alone becomes, for Bamba, a metaphysical exile: a sacred journey within, to the imperceptible core of one's disease.

Like Bamba, Murids abroad also speak of their diasporic itineraries as routes towards profound religious education. Pape Birama Diop, who has lived in Italy for twenty years, states,

> I went to Europe seeking wealth. But in Europe I can say that I found something better than the wealth that I sought . . . I found the shaykh there. I am Senegalese but I found the shaykh in Europe. In the *dahiras,* I learned a great deal from the disciples . . . what I learned about the shaykh in Europe, I did not know when I was here in Senegal . . . it's the values of service, religious teachings, reciprocity, the respect of the human individual. (Pape Birama Diop, representative of 18 Safar, interview with author, Touba, January 9, 2012)[79]

Abroad, many Murids report spending more time at *dahira* meetings than they would have if in Senegal. In the *dahiras,* disciples study Bamba's messages, discuss concrete projects for the development of Bamba's city, collect financial offerings, and sing and listen to *qaṣāʾid.* Some begin

[78] Babou, *Fighting the Greater Jihad,* 135. For the poem cited by Babou, see Amadou Bamba Mbacké, *Jazāʾ al-shakūr* (*Tribute to the Worthy of Recognition*). Translated into French and edited by the Association of Murid Students of University Cheikh Anta Diop of Dakar, Dakar, n.d., 19.

[79] 18 Safar is a federation of five *dahiras* in the Lombardy region of Italy: Touba Lecco, Touba Monza, Touba Bezana, Touba Mariano, Touba Erba.

singing in *kureels* while abroad, where they only listened in Senegal. Away from the *dahiras,* Murids enjoy the freedom to read sacred texts that solitude can offer.

> Here in Senegal, for me it's not easy. The family . . . you come and you begin [to read], someone enters . . . that's why I have heard it said that the shaykh preferred solitude. Sometimes it is better to relocate in order to better concentrate, because by yourself you profit from many advantages . . . sometimes in life, one needs moments of intimacy with the Creator. (Pape Birama Diop, interview with author, Touba, January 9, 2012)

The social obligations of the worldly home can detract from concentrating on Bamba's teachings. Abdou Karim Mbengue believes that these distractions are present even in Touba.

> When I am in Touba, there are preoccupations. The family . . . but when I am in Italy, I work, and after work I do nothing. I take care of myself, my priorities—and that is Serigne Touba, to know, learn, and read the Qur'an or the *qaṣāʾid.* I don't have any other concern. (Abdou Karim Mbengue, representative of Toubatoscano, interview with author, Touba, January 9, 2012)[80]

While all of the Murids abroad interviewed for this study wish to return to Senegal, they speak of their extended diasporic itineraries with optimism and appreciation, as opportunities to dwell in the sacred writings that elevate the soul.

In his *qaṣāʾid,* Bamba reconfigures exile, the forced journey outward, into a process of purification, a blessed journey inward. And perhaps this is the reason why Bamba fixed the date of the *magal* as on the anniversary of his deportation to Gabon. In choosing the 18th of Safar as the date of the *magal,* Bamba declares that the cause of celebration is the entry into isolation, the embarking on a difficult and dangerous journey for the sake of spiritual purification. The day one commits to the sacred journey within—to probing the depths of one's disease—this is the day of celebration. While the exterior of the *magal* is characterized by the commotion,

[80] Toubatoscana is a federation of multiple *dahiras* in the Tuscany region of Italy. Its website gives an idea of the activities engaged in by Murid *dahiras* in the diaspora; see www.toubatoscana.com.

volume, and revelry of any large religious gathering, at its heart is a specific story which claims that the purposeful entry into suffering is the beginning of joy.

During the Grand Magal, diasporic Murids celebrating Bamba's exile recast their own displacement as an act of piety modeled after the saint himself. In the *magal,* Murids renew through their contemporary travel the foundational stories of faith. Of the *magal,* piety, and diaspora, the president of Dahira Moukhadimatoul Khidma of Philadelphia states:

> When the shaykh was deported, he was facing hardship because he was taken outside of his country and his family into a country where he didn't know anything. But he took it like a blessing, because he said, "God had answered my prayer, because this will enable me to devote all of my life to worshipping [him]. And that is a challenge and I want to accept it." And, in fact, that's where the Muridiyya has known a big expansion, thanks to the big travel, the big deportation. After his return, some people were celebrating because they missed him. They were happy to see him, but he said, "No, this is not a day of celebration. The day of celebration was the day when I was deported." (Mbacké Thioune, interview with author, Philadelphia, November 4, 2010)

Today, there are tens of thousands of Murids living in diasporic communities abroad. Individuals, goods, and media circulate rapidly within the vigorous diasporic networks, which are singularly attuned to the political and economic goals of the Muridiyya as a whole. The Murid leadership supports the migration of able believers, as "each Murid is an ambassador of Serigne Touba abroad"[81] and can contribute to the dissemination of Bamba's message and the international expansion of the religious community. Murids working abroad are also responsible for impressive development projects that are making Touba Senegal's most rapidly modernizing city. These diasporic projects include schools and research centers, electricity infrastructure and water management, public health initiatives, recycling and environmental preservation. Here, it is worth noting two completed projects by Matlaboul Fawzaini, a transnational *dahira* of disciples mostly in Europe and North America:[82] the first is the hospital

[81] Abdou Karim Mbengue, interview with author, Touba, January 9, 2012.

[82] Both the *dahira* and the hospital Matlaboul Fawzaini are named after *Maṭlab al-fawzayn,* the poem Bamba wrote upon first setting foot in Touba.

Matlaboul Fawzaini, funded by more than $10 million in contributions from diasporic Murids;[83] the second, a modern morgue conforming to the principles of Islam, because "when they die, all Murids prefer to return here, to be transported to Touba."[84]

In leaving Touba for the sake of strengthening the Muridiyya, the contemporary diaspora is an expression of the Sufi conception of exile as piety—an exile that is exemplified by Bamba's imprisonment in Gabon. Though ritual travel to the spiritual home in Touba is central to Murid theology, migration away from that home has come to constitute a sacred journey in itself. When embarked upon with purpose and religious remembrance, the journey away from Touba can—like the journey to Touba—embody a return to the spiritual home, to the *baraka* of the saint and to closeness with God.

Conclusion

For those who would prefer to live in Touba, to return to Touba, to be buried in Touba, the diasporic life is "like an exile, these trials. To be far from your family, to be far from your parents, to be far from your sons, is already a sacrifice . . . it's for sake of the love that we have for Serigne Touba."[85] That the poetic messages of Ahmadu Bamba are spread through the voices of *dahira* members, and that the projects of the Muridiyya are financed through the work of their hands—this is the balm that soothes the aches of traveling Murid feet. And indeed, Bamba was, himself, never able to make his abode the blessed city of Touba. Fearful of his ever-increasing popularity and the large conversions to Islam that he generated, the French colonial government prohibited Bamba from establishing himself in Touba and adopted a policy of continually uprooting the Sufi shaykh. Bamba endured two long periods of exile, the first to Gabon from 1895 to 1902, the second to Mauritania from 1903 to 1907. In addition to these two periods, Bamba was forcefully relocated every few years to different localities within the colony in efforts to disrupt the community of believers growing around him. Unable within his lifetime to live in his beloved city, Bamba would finally return to Touba when he was buried there in 1927.

83 See Guèye, *Touba,* 249–58; and Ellen E. Foley and Cheikh Anta Babou, "Diaspora, Faith, and Science: Building a Mouride Hospital in Senegal," *African Affairs* 110, no. 438 (2010): 79.

84 Pape Birama Diop, interview with author, Touba, January 9, 2012.

85 Abdou Karim Mbengue, interview with author, Touba, January 9, 2012.

Bamba, however, did not look upon his compulsory removal from Touba as a cause of misery. Exile afforded him time to pray, to meditate, to write, to leave the things of this world in concentration on the divine alone. Exile brought him closer to God, closer to the *ṭūbā* of the Qur'an—the felicity and bliss of a life righteously lived.

In his *qaṣīda Midādī* (*My Ink*), written during exile in Mauritania, Bamba speaks of his verses as an act of devotion that pleases God.[86] "My ink and my pen are devoted to He who parted the sea, as He prevailed over Satan and anguish and ignorance."[87] He further connects his praise of God through ink and pen with sacred journey and salvation from suffering. "Allah has shortened for me my spiritual journey by his grace . . . I have shortened the journey of the saints the very moment that I made his praise."[88] Commemorating the relationship between poetry, journeys, and divine grace, *Midādī* eloquently captures the current global imaginary of pilgrimage—an imaginary that includes diasporic paths expanding Murid influence abroad in addition to ritual returns to the physical home of the Muridiyya in Touba. While comprising variegated geographic terrain and diverse sociopolitical contexts, both journey to Touba and journey away from Touba are mediated by the sounds of *qaṣāʾid.* The singing of *qaṣāʾid* also connects those two journeys, sonically performing the link between the memory of Bamba's blessed exile, the Murid traditions of pilgrimage, and the contemporary reality of diaspora. Despite the differences in the physical destinations, the Murid communities of Senegal, China, Europe, and North America celebrate their religious journeys with the same sung verses. They accomplish their divergent but similarly faithful pilgrimages by singing the same poetry.

References

Babou, Cheikh Anta. "Brotherhood Solidarity, Education and Migration: The Role of the Dahiras Among the Murid Muslim Community of New York." *African Affairs* 403 (2002): 151–70.

[86] I am grateful to Dame Diene for introducing me to *Midādī* with his own beautiful voice in Philadelphia.

[87] Ahmadu Bamba Mbacké, *Waqānī, Midādī, Yasurru* (Dakar: Impression Edition Islamique, n.d.), 9.

[88] *Midādī,* 12. For an audiovisual recording, see *Midādī,* Hizbut-Tarqiyyah, 2007, http://www.youtube.com/watch?v=9EuYIyjdQtU&playnext=1&list=PL4191C7533C1C2A4F&feature=results_video.

———. *Fighting the Greater Jihad: Amadu Bamba and the Founding of the Muridiyya of Senegal, 1853–1913.* Athens: Ohio University Press, 2007.
———. "Urbanizing Mystical Islam: Making Murid Space in the Cities of Senegal." *International Journal of African Historical Studies* 40, no. 2 (2007): 197–223.
Bava, Sophie, and Cheikh Guèye. "Le grand magal de Touba: Exil prophétique, migration et pèlerinage au sein du mouridisme." *Social Compass* 48, no. 3 (2001): 421–38.
Bithell, Caroline. *Transported by Song: Corsican Voices from Oral Tradition to World Stage.* Lanham, Md.: Scarecrow, 2007.
Carter, Donald Martin. *States of Grace: Senegalese in Italy and the New Europe Immigration.* Minneapolis: University of Minnesota Press, 1997.
Charry, Eric. *Mande Music: Traditional and Modern Music of the Maninka and Mandinka of Western Africa.* Chicago: University of Chicago Press, 2000.
Copans, Jean. *Les marabouts de l'arachide.* Paris: L'Harmattan, 1988.
Coulon, Christian. "The Grand Magal in Touba: A Religious Festival of the Mouride Brotherhood of Senegal." *African Affairs* 98, no. 391 (1999): 195–210.
Cruise O'Brien, Donal. *The Mourides of Senegal: The Political and Economic Organization of an Islamic Brotherhood.* London: Oxford University Press, 1971.
de Jong, Ferdinand. "Remembering the Nation: The Mourid Maggal in Saint Louis, Senegal." *Cahiers d'Études Africaines* 197 (2010): 123–51.
Diop, Abdoul Malal. "Traduction et commentaire du Viatique des Jeunes d'Ahmadou Bamba." Third-cycle doctoral thesis, University of Dakar, Dakar, 1985.
Diop, Momar Coumba. "Fonctions et activités des dahiras mourides urbains (Sénégal)." *Cahiers d'Études Africaines* 21, nos. 81–83 (1982): 79–91.
———. "La confrérie mouride: Organisation politique et mode d'implantation urbaine." Third-cycle doctoral thesis, University of Lyon 2, 1980.
Diouf, Mamadou, "The Senegalese Murid Trade Diaspora and the Making of a Vernacular Cosmopolitanism," trans. Steven Rendall, *Public Culture* 12, no. 3 (2000): 679–702.
Dumont, Fernand. *La pensée religieuse d'Amadou Bamba.* Dakar: Nouvelles editions africaines, 1975.
Ebin, Victoria. "International Networks of Trading Diaspora: The Mourides of Senegal Abroad." In *La ville à guichets fermés: Itinéraires, réseaux et insertion urbaine,* ed. Philippe Antoine and Abdoulaye Bara Diop, 323–36. Paris: ORSTOM, 1995.
Foley, Ellen E., and Cheikh Anta Babou. "Diaspora, Faith, and Science: Building a Mouride Hospital in Senegal." *African Affairs* 110, no. 438 (2010): 75–95.

Frishkopf, Michael. "Tarab in the Mysic Sufi Chant of Egypt." In *Colors of Enchantment: Visual and Performing Arts of the Middle East,* ed. Sherifa Zuhur, 233–69. Cairo: American University in Cairo Press, 2001.

Hale, Thomas A. *Griots and Griottes: Masters of Words and Music.* Bloomington: Indiana University Press, 1998.

———. "Islam and the Griots in West Africa: Bridging the Gap Between Traditions." *Africana Journal* 13 (1982): 84–90.

Harris, Laura Arnston. "The Play of Ambiguity in Praise-Song Performance: A Definition of the Genre Through an Examination of Its Practice in Northern Sierra Leone." Ph.D. dissertation, Indiana University, 1992.

Kapchan, Deborah. *Traveling Spirit Masters: Moroccan Gnawa Trance and Music in the Global Marketplace.* Middleton, Conn.: Wesleyan University Press, 2007.

Malcomson, Scott L. "West of Eden: The Mouride Ethic and the Spirit of Capitalism." *Transition* 71 (1996): 24–43.

Mbacké, Amadou Bamba. *Jazā' al-shakūr* (*Tribute to the Worthy of Recognition*). Translated into French and edited by the Association of Murid Students of University Cheikh Anta Diop of Dakar. Dakar, n.d.

McLaughlin, Fiona. "'In the Name of God I Will Sing Again, Mawdo Malick the Good': Popular Music and Senegalese Sufi Tariqas." *Journal of Religion in Africa* 30, no. 2 (2000): 191–207.

———. "Islam and Popular Music in Senegal: The Emergence of a 'New Tradition.'" *Africa* 67, no. 4 (1997): 560–81.

Nelson, Kristina. *The Art of Reciting the Qur'an.* New York: University in Cairo Press, 2001.

Qureshi, Regula. *Sufi Music of India and Pakistan: Sound, Context, and Meaning in Qawwali.* Chicago: University of Chicago Press, 1997.

Racy, A. J. *Making Music in the Arab World: The Culture and Artistry of Tarab.* Oxford: Oxford University Press, 2002.

Robinson, David. *Paths of Accommodation: Muslim Societies and French Colonial Authorities in Senegal and Mauritania, 1880–1920.* Athens: Ohio University Press, 2000.

Rommen, Timothy. *Mek Some Noise: Gospel Music and the Ethics of Style in Trinidad.* Berkeley: University of California Press, 2007.

Ross, Eric. *Sufi City: Urban Design and Archetypes in Touba.* Rochester, N.Y.: University of Rochester Press, 2006.

Samb, Amar. *Essai sur la contribution du Sénégal à la literature d'expression arabe.* Dakar: IFAN, 1972.

———. "Touba et son 'Magal.'" *Bulletin de l'IFAN* (Dakar) 31 (1969): 733–53.

Sperl, Stefan, and Christopher Shackle, eds. *Qasida Poetry in Islamic Asia and Africa,* 2 volumes. Leiden: E. J. Brill, 1996.

Stone, Ruth M. *Dried Millet Breaking: Time, Words, and Songs in the Wòi Epic of the Kpelle.* Bloomington: Indiana University Press, 1988.

Tang, Patricia. 2007. *Masters of the Sabar: Wolof Griot Percussionists of Senegal.* Philadelphia: Temple University Press.

Villalón, Leonardo A. "Sufi Rituals as Rallies: Religious Ceremonies in the Politics of Senegalese State-Society Relations." *Comparative Politics* 26, no. 4 (1994): 415–37.

Kadhis Courts in Kenya's Constitutional Review (1998–2010): A Changing Approach to Politics and State Among Kenyan Muslim Leaders

Abdulkader Tayob, UNIVERSITY OF CAPE TOWN

DOI: 10.5192/215409930401103

ABSTRACT

Debate over Kadhis courts in the constitutional review process (1998–2010) in Kenya antagonized relations between Muslims and Christians. Generally, Muslims found themselves on the defensive as some Christian groups mounted a sustained campaign against the place of Kadhis courts in the constitution. This paper presents Muslim responses to this public debate in the larger framework of Muslims in the nation-state. Since the 1990s, the Kenyan state was engaged in a search for a new politics. This paper turns to this question, and finds that beneath the rhetoric about Kadhis courts, Muslim responses were focused on politics. They were placing the Kadhis court debate within the larger question of how Muslims relate to the nation-state of Kenya.

Scholars frequently mention the marginalization of Muslims in the body politic of Kenya. Alamin Mazrui argued that Moi's extensive reign from 1978 to 2002 employed an idiosyncratic Christian symbolism to inscribe the nation and support authoritarian rule. In this national imagination, according to Mazrui, religious minorities like the Muslims could not be accommodated.[1] Cussac supported this perspective of post-colonial national

[1] A. Mazrui, "Ethnicity and Pluralism: The Politicization of Religion in Kenya," *Journal of Muslim Minority Affairs* 14, no. 1 (1993): 191–201.

Islamic Africa, VOL. 4, NO. 1, 2013. ISSN 2154-0993. www.islamicafricajournal.org

leaders in their inclination towards Christianity.[2] Constantin and Haynes have reminded us that some Muslims benefited from this arrangement in the post-colonial state, or at least took advantage of authoritarianism where possible. In support of this view, they have documented a common pattern of Muslim accommodation to post-colonial East African states. In particular, they argued that the various national Muslim organizations worked with ruling governments and parties, irrespective of their political philosophies and ideologies.[3] In Kenya in particular, the national Muslim organization leading this political accommodation was the Supreme Council of Kenya Muslims (SUPKEM) that was founded in 1973,[4] and officially recognized by the Kenyan government as the representative of Kenyan Muslims in 1979.[5] It is not surprising, therefore, that a number of groups and individuals have emerged in the Kenyan political arena since the 1990s that questioned this politics of accommodation. They targeted, in particular, the kind of politics pursued by SUPKEM, blaming them for the continued marginalization of Muslims in the country. The most spectacular of these have been the Islamic Party of Kenya that attempted in vain to register itself as a political party in 1992. Led by a former street preacher, Khalid Balala, it did not become a recognized force among Muslims and Kenyans. However, it demonstrated the deep hostility felt towards the state and current political representatives for Muslims.[6]

These two contrasting perspectives on the Kenyan nation-state will be used as a background to analyzing Muslim political views on the Kadhis

[2] A. Cussac, "Muslims and Politics in Kenya: The Issue of the Kadhis' Courts in the Constitution Review Process," *Journal of Muslim Minority Affairs* (2008). See also Kresse for a different perspective on this marginalization: K. Kresse, "Muslim Politics in Postcolonial Kenya: Negotiating Knowledge on the Double-Periphery," *Journal of the Royal Anthropological Institute* 15 (2009): 76–94.

[3] F. Constantin, "Charisma and the Crisis of Power in East Africa," in *Charisma and Brotherhood in African Islam*, ed. D. B. C. O'Brien and C. Coulon (Oxford: Clarendon, 1988); F. Constantin, "Leadership, Muslim Identities, and East African Politics: Tradition, Bureaucratisation and Communication," in *Muslim Identity and Social Change in Sub-Saharan Africa*, ed. L. Brenner (London: Hurst, 1993); F. Constantin, "Muslims and Politics: The Attempts to Create Muslim National Organisations in Tanzania, Uganda and Kenya," in *Religion and Politics in East Africa: The Period Since Independence*, ed. H. B. Hansen and M. Twaddle, Eastern African Studies (London: James Curry, 1995); J. Haynes, "Islam and Democracy in East Africa," *Democratization* 13, no. 3 (2006): 490–507.

[4] *Jamia Masjidi Nairobi,* http://www.islamkenya.com/html/supkem.html.

[5] A. Oded, *Islam and Politics in Kenya* (London: Lynne Rienner, 2000).

[6] Ibid.

courts during the constitutional review process. From the mid-1990s to 2010, Kenyans engaged in an extensive public debate over a new constitution for the country. A number of contentious issues emerged, but the role of Kadhis courts in the constitution and in the Kenyan state structure became at times the most controversial of these among Muslims and Christians. In this article, I examine this controversy from the perspective of diverse Muslim leaders. I present their views on the Kadhis courts and the Kenyan constitution, and locate them within the broader history of Muslims and politics in post-colonial Kenya. Muslim views on Kadhis courts become more salient when placed within this longer history of engagement with the state and public life. The Kadhis courts issue did not produce a new political perspective for Kenyan Muslims. Muslim views, however, suggest a search for an alternative to both the politics of accommodation and the politics of resistance. Both these options are reflected in the interviews, but another path is considered and imagined by some Muslims in the Kenyan state. Moreover, I think it is important to locate this discussion within the much wider debate on Muslim political thinking in the modern world. Kenyan Muslims, it will be shown, grapple with the demands of a pluralist state on the one hand, and ideas about Islamic politics on the other.

Constitutional Review and Kadhis Courts

Like many countries in Africa, the impact of the end of Cold War was felt in Kenyan politics. President Moi, who had been ruling the country since 1978, announced the liberalization of the political sphere in 1992. The announcement of multiparty politics sparked an immediate and hopeful reaction among civil society and religious groups. Many Kenyans took advantage of this liberal atmosphere, including Muslims who formed a political party. Initiatives were taken to persuade the government to change and relax its hold on power. Eventually, many movements were initiated among civil society groups to demand a new constitution for Kenya, focused on the decentralization of the powers of the executive.

Public pressure led to the adoption of the Kenya Review Commission (Amendment) Act of 1998, a first step in a process towards a review of the constitution of the country. The act of 1998 was a commitment to change the foundation of the Kenyan state, beginning with the appointment of a commission to guide the process. Around this time, a number of civil society and religious groups formed a pressure group called the Ufungamano initiative outside Parliament to keep the constitutional review in the public eye. This group feared that the review process might be limited to parliamentarians, and ignore the Kenyan public. By December 1999, this initiative was formalized and formed a People's Commission, and pressured the government to pass the Kenya Review Act of 2000. The act constituted a fifteen-member commission of parliamentary members, which was amended in June 2001 to include ten members from the People's Commission. The final commission, called the Kenya Constitutional Review Commission, held hearings throughout the length and breadth of the country, and presented a first draft for discussion. In 2004, this draft was debated at meetings held outside Nairobi, the capital city of Kenya. A new draft of the constitution was formulated and presented to the Attorney-General Amos Wako. The so-called Wako Draft was presented to a national referendum in 2005, but rejected by most Kenyans. After a disastrous national election in 2007, a Committee of Experts was formed to prepare another draft of the constitution. A Harmonized Draft (2009), duly revised in 2010, was presented to Kenyans in a national referendum in August 2010.[7] This time, a new constitution was accepted by an overwhelming majority of voters.

The constitutional review process generated intense debate among Kenyans. Most of the fundamental issues turned around the devolution of power throughout the country. However, the presence of Kadhis courts in the constitution divided Christian and Muslim religious leaders, and appeared to threaten the review process itself. The Kadhis courts had been part of the legal framework of the country since the foundation of the modern Kenyan state. They were responsible for adjudicating disputes among Muslims in personal status law relating to marriage, divorce, and testaments. During the national consultations of the Kenya Constitutional Review Commission, some Muslims expressed a desire for an appeals process within the Kadhis courts before cases were taken to higher national courts. Others wanted more training for kadhis, and some desired the jurisdiction of the Kadhis courts to be expanded to small claims involving financial transactions. A few Muslims even wanted the jurisdiction of Kadhis courts to include criminal matters.[8]

[7] J. A. Chesworth, "Kadhi's Courts in Kenya: Reactions and Responses," in *Constitutional Review in Kenya and Kadhis Courts: Selected Papers Presented at the Workshop 20 March 2010*, ed. A. Tayob and J. Wandera (Cape Town: Centre for Contemporary Islam, 2011).

[8] A. I. Hassan, "Working Document for the Constitution of Kenya Review Commission on the Kadhi's Courts, Chief Kadhi and Kadhis," http://www.kenyaconstitution.org/docs/07d046.htm.

A number of churches objected to the presence of the Kadhis courts in the draft constitutions. Some argued that Islam was given special privilege in the constitution to the exclusion of other religions. They objected to the Kadhis courts entrenched within the legal structure of the country, giving Islam a unique place in the constitution. Others were concerned that such demands were the first step towards the Islamization of the country, fueled by what they regarded as a radicalization of Muslims in East Africa and elsewhere.[9] Many of the churches were not advocating a neutral, secular state for Kenya, but had their own ideas of infusing religious values and symbols in the state of Kenya.[10] There were a number of Muslim responses to the debate. To some extent, they were mostly reactions to the criticisms leveled by Christian leaders and institutions. However, Muslims were also responding to the broader political context within which the Kadhis courts dispute emerged. This article presents Muslim responses to the Kadhis courts in this broader political context.

I conducted about forty interviews in 2003 and 2010 with activists, lawyers, judges, Christian and Muslim academics, religious scholars, and kadhis on the Kadhis courts and the constitutional review process. I initially focused my interviews on the role, meaning, and function of Kadhis courts in a comparative African legal context. Each of the interviews presented deep insights on the meaning of the Kadhis courts for Muslims in the country. While the judicial function of the Kadhis courts was taken for granted, their political role and meaning also elicited interesting responses. I then decided to look at the interviews with a focus on the politics of Kenya, without completely ignoring the judicial sphere around which the views were presented. Hence, I decided to focus on clusters of

---

[9] K. Maina, "Islamophobia Among Christians and Its Challenges in Entrenchment of Kadhis Courts in Kenya," in *Constitutional Review in Kenya and Kadhis Courts: Selected Papers Presented at the Workshop 20 March 2010*, ed. A. Tayob and J. Wandera (Cape Town: Centre for Contemporary Islam, 2011); J. Wandera, "Anglican Responses to Kadhis Courts in Kenya," in *Constitutional Review in Kenya and Kadhis Courts: Selected Papers Presented at the Workshop 20 March 2010*, ed. A. Tayob and J. Wandera (Cape Town: Centre for Contemporary Islam, 2011).

[10] A. I. Tayob, "The Demand for Sharī'ah in African Democratisation Processes: Pitfalls or Opportunities?" in *Comparative Perspectives on Shari'ah in Nigeria*, ed. P. Ostien et al. (Ibadan: Spectrum Books, 2005). See also the report produced by the Kenya church, "Recommendations to the Constitution of Kenya Review Commission on the Proposed Draft Constitution of the Republic of Kenya," *The Kenya Church* (2002). A pamphlet distributed in Kenya.

interviews with kadhis, activists, and members of the Kenyan judiciary. They represent the nodal points of the debate among Kenyans in general, and Kenyan Muslims in particular. Kadhis were the obvious starting point, even though they did not directly get involved in the public debate. One kadhi informed me in 2010 that he consciously decided not to engage the public controversy in order to maintain his integrity as a judge and a civil servant. I interviewed four kadhis, one of which I present in detail below. Activists were the major protagonists of the public debate on Kadhis courts, and I present the view of two such individuals to illustrate their perspective. And the legal fraternity was my third cluster of interviewees since they dealt directly with the kadhis and with the broader legal system of the country. I present the views of a lawyer in Nairobi who also had an Islamic legal background. One unintended consequence of my choice was that I present in this article interviews conducted only in 2003. This does not imply that nothing much had changed between 2003 and 2010. My analysis and the focus for this article only became clear to me in 2010, and I read the 2003 interviews with this later perspective. The interviewees do not represent the views of all Kenyan Muslims, but bring up common issues and perspectives on the politics of the country.

The interviews suggest how Kenyans conceptualize the Kadhis courts as part of the constitutional review. As the latter was intended to change the political framework of the country, such Muslim responses were not unexpected. I offer an analysis of some of the information gathered, and place them within the general framework on Muslims and politics in Kenya. In the concluding discussion, I also place these reflections within general reflections on Muslims, the modern state, and politics.

From Marginalization to Civic Engagement

Abdul Hamid Slatch and Abdulrahman Wandati[11] were leading members of activist organizations in Kenya. They were members of a Muslim Consultative Council founded in 1997 to represent Muslims in Kenyan public life in general, and in the constitutional process in particular. Slatch was born in Nairobi in 1942, and pursued business and management studies in Kenya and Islamic studies in Kenya and Malaysia. He was one of the founders of the Young Muslim Association first registered in 1964.[12]

[11] A. H. Slatch and A. Wandati, interview by A. I. Tayob, Nairobi, June 17, 2003.

[12] http://tymagmch.blogspot.com/2006/07/yma.html.

He was also an executive member of the central mosque in Nairobi. Wandati (born 1961) hails from western Kenya, and completed high school in Uganda. He followed up with studies in Pakistan (Islamabad), Portugal, and the United States as a Democracy Scholar at the Les Aspin Center for Government in Washington, D.C. Both Slatch and Wandati held positions in various Islamic and Kenyan public bodies. Wandati was a founder-member of the short-lived Islamic Party founded in 1992.[13]

Slatch and Wandati were deeply involved in the constitutional review process from 1996. They recognized the review process as an opportunity for Muslims to escape their marginalization in Kenya since independence. They believed that Muslims should accept some of the responsibility for marginalization by refusing secular education and failing to acquire the necessary skills for a modern state. But the situation at the end of the twentieth century was different, they said, and Muslims had no excuse not to assert themselves this time around. It is not surprising that Wandati earlier founded the Islamic Party to represent the interests of Muslims.

Slatch and Wandati believed that they were the first religious activists to approach Anglican and later other Christian leaders to form a civil society group for a new constitution. They developed their civic engagement that later came to be known as the Ufungamano initiative and was recognized by state and society. From 1996, they were making a constructive contribution to the future constitution of the country. In 2003, however, Slatch and Wandati were devastated when their Christian colleagues rejected Kadhis courts in the new constitution. With other Muslims, they then withdrew from the Ufungamano, but kept a vigilant presence in civic and public life. They cooperated with Christian groups, but witnessed the rise of a strong Christian presence in Kenyan politics. In search of votes and support, many politicians in their view turned government activities into Christian gatherings. Slatch had this to say about one government meeting:

> Last week Tuesday there was breakfast prayers meeting for the city council, the councilors, organized by the mayor. Again, it was this Christian Leadership Development initiative . . . Fortunately I was invited to attend, but unfortunately I told them I could not go. Because we discussed,

[13] A. Oded, "Islamic Extremism in Kenya: The Rise and Fall of Sheikh Khalid Balala," *Journal of Religion in Africa* 26, no. 4 (1996): 407.

> me and Wandati . . . he said "No, this is a political process, you [should] go!" [But I said] "No, it's not a political process, it is a prayer meeting." How do you expect me to stand and you know sing hymns with them, and . . . the program said first reading from the Old Testament, second reading from the New Testament, singing of hymns, I will be very uncomfortable . . . So I decided not to go. So I received a message from the deputy who happens to be a Muslim, they said, oh there has been some kind of talk [on political matters].

This lengthy quote illustrates how Slatch and Wandati saw government activity closely related to Christian symbols. At the same time, it shows how Muslims were struggling to find a way of negotiating their political engagement with it.

With this understanding of current politics in Kenya, Wandati offered his reflections on the Kenyan state. He suggested that, given the strong religious conviction of Kenyans, a secular state was not an option. Kenya should rather define itself as an "ecumenical" state, a concept first proposed by the internationally renowned Kenyan scholar Ali Mazrui. An ecumenical state, according to Wandati, was one wherein "benefits that accrue from the state . . . should not be based on the fact that these individuals, or this community of citizens are subscribed to a particular religious order." An ecumenical state "recognizes" the particular worship in which religious groups engage in, and then "goes out of its way to facilitate all its infrastructure" so "that all the different religious groupings within the country . . . enjoy . . . religious worship or practice to the fullest extent." Wandati was adamant that the Kadhis courts could not be removed from the new constitution.

Interestingly, Wandati did not regard the service offered by Kadhis courts as part of the religious symbols of Kenyan Muslims: "We do not regard . . . the Kadhis court in Kenya as a religious institution. We regard it as part of the judiciary." Wandati was aware of Kadhis performing a range of religious activities, in addition to their judicial duties. He thought, however, that such functions should henceforth be performed by a new office within the Muslim community:

> Now all the things the Muslims are toying with, is that we then need to have a mufti [jurisprudent in shari'a]. And if they do have a mufti then what will be his role, we have never experienced this. I know that in Uganda they do have a mufti.

Wandati went on:

> That's my understanding . . . the mufti will be a people's leader, if we do have a mufti here, he will that one who we regard as the shaykh [an elder or recognized religious leader].

The ecumenical state of Kenya would support all religious activities. For Muslims, moreover, a mufti would oversee religious activities. Wandati also revealed a distinct understanding of the Kadhis courts. They should remain an integral part of the judiciary, but Kenyan Muslims needed a different *religious* representative for the Kenyan nation and state. His last remark seemed to lead in the direction of the Supreme Council of Kenya Muslims. Wandati did not discuss the umbrella organization, but here seemed to suggest that an alternative organization be founded to engage the state and represent Muslims in Kenya.

In summary, we see Slatch and Wandati engaged in civil activism for a new constitution that would end the marginalization of Muslims in the country. However, they were shocked by how the political space was overtaken by Christian churches, with the collusion of Christian political leaders. They offered the ecumenical state as an alternative to both the secular and the Christian-dominated state. Equally importantly, the idea of an ecumenical state was also an opportunity to rethink established Muslim approaches to the state. And one of these was a redefinition of the Kadhis courts as part of the judiciary, excised from its religious function. And the state would support different religious rituals.

Secular State and Religious Authority

I turn now to Muhammad Khamis,[14] who studied Islamic law in the Sudan, and then completed his legal training in Nairobi. He owned a successful legal practice in Nairobi, and occasionally represented clients at Kadhis courts. Khamis's interview covered a range of aspects, including some of those raised by Slatch and Wandati. He also discussed the issue of the Kenyan state, and reflected on the reforms required of the Kadhis courts. With regard to the latter, he believed that lawyers and attorneys should take some of the responsibility for how the courts functioned: "We are

[14] Muhammad Khamis (original name changed), interview by A. I. Tayob, Nairobi, June 19, 2003.

really heavily to blame for the state that the Kadhis courts find themselves in today." Clearly, Khamis was not satisfied with the working of the courts. In light of his proposed reform of these courts, Khamis also turned to the distinction between the religious and legal function of the Kadhis courts. Understandably, given his legal background, he did not propose the appointment of a mufti to take over national religious decisions for Muslims but pointed to a concrete problem faced by Kenyans.

Khamis was not in favor of an ecumenical state, but veered towards support for a secular state under the particular circumstances facing Kenya. He began with a response that he would like to live in an Islamic state in Kenya. Upon probing his response, he then admitted that he could not imagine living in an Islamic state such as Saudi Arabia. Iran was a more likely possibility: "Iran, maybe, maybe, but right now I have not really focused my attention on living, living outside this country." When asked about a secular option, he responded that both Christians and Muslims would not support such an idea. Secularists in both communities in Kenya were isolated, according to Khamis. Nevertheless, he believed that a secular option was inevitable in Kenya. He was critical of the secularism supported by Christian leaders, suggesting that it was merely a ruse to oppose the Muslims: "Christians are pushing for a secular state just to counter the Muslim position as far as the Kadhis courts are concerned." What they really wanted, according to Khamis, was contained in a document that the Kenya Church, a coalition of Christian Evangelical churches opposed to the Kadhis courts, issued in 2002. Among other things, the document declared that the Kenya church wanted to "ensure that the final Constitution not only reflects the wishes of Kenyans, but also the eternal purposes of God."[15] According to Khamis, then, Christians were promoting a religious state for Kenya. In response, Khamis believed that a secular state was the best option for Muslims: "The reality is that we are better off as compared to living in a strictly Christian state—we are better off living in a secular state than living in a Christian state as such."

Khamis then moved to a discussion of the Kadhis courts. His main focus here were the kinds of reforms necessary. First, the "structures and the jurisdiction of the Kadhis courts" needed to be enhanced. On one level, this was related to the training and appointment of the kadhis which the Kenya Constitutional Review Commission heard in general:

---

[15] "Recommendations to the Constitution of Kenya Review Commission on the Proposed Draft Constitution of the Republic of Kenya," *The Kenya Church* (2002).

"on qualifications of the Kadhis . . . I think that . . . the current crop that we have is not really up to date." This sentiment came up frequently in a number of other interviews as well, and was in some respects supported by some of the kadhis. Khamis himself specified his remark by mentioning the need for training in reforms in Islamic law. I particularly asked him if the issue of national or international human rights was relevant in the discussion on Kadhis courts. His responses may be divided into two. First, he argued that the right to go to the Kadhis courts was guaranteed for Muslims only. Non-Muslims were not compelled to live under shari'a:

> The law applicable as I said in the Kadhis court would be Islamic law, and as a Muslim you are supposed to . . . to be happy that the law has been applied . . . but if you are not a Muslim and law is applied onto you, you could talk about infringement of your right . . . in my entire practice I have not come across a case where a party has claimed that their rights are being infringed in the Kadhis court, just because they don't profess the Muslim religion.

The state was not imposing Islamic law on its citizens. Muslim citizens were turning to the kadhis to seek redress against other Muslims who were depriving them of their rights in terms of Islamic law. Moreover, Khamis explained that Islamic law was a matter of horizontal civil relations, in which human rights need not apply.

But Khamis did explore a second dimension of rights in terms of the interpretation of Islamic law that may directly and indirectly affect the Kadhis courts. He was clear that Muslims in general and kadhis in particular needed to think about the application of Islamic law in modern contexts. Since social contexts had changed, some of the rules in Islamic law needed to change as well: "I think there ought to be development of . . . law, Islamic law, in the sense that . . . we are living in a different, completely different world from the world that the Prophet lived in." Specifically, he mentioned two examples in this regard. The first was the law of evidence in which, according to certain issues in Islamic law, for "the evidence of one man, you have to have the evidence of two women." In Kadhis courts in Kenya, however, Khamis quickly reminded me that the Kenyan procedure on this issue did not disadvantage women:

> [In] the present system according to the Kadhis Act, it, it clearly states that there should be no discrimination on the evidence, the evidence is not

> based on the number of people that give the evidence . . . it basically means that the evidence of a man is the same as the evidence of the woman.

On this point, at least, it seems that the shari'a had in fact already developed for Kenyan Muslims. In his second point, Khamis referred to the social discrimination faced by some Kenyan Muslim women. He mentioned a custom in the northeast where women were not supposed to sit on chairs. He accepted that this was a cultural practice restricted to this region, but admitted that it could be an interpretation "of a certain verse of the Qur'an which says that men, for example, are superior to women." This second example was not specifically related to Kadhis courts, but Khamis mentioned it in response to the possible conflict between Islamic law and human rights. He seemed to present this cultural practice as a social norm that deprives women of equal rights. Moreover, he suggested that this social practice may be justified in terms of Qur'anic verses. Khamis did not pursue this line of thinking, as it opened up questions of modern interpretations of Islamic law and its general absence in the Kadhis court debate. Unlike debates elsewhere on the relevance of Islamic law in modern societies, the Kenyan dispute over Kadhis courts was dominated by political questions. Even Khamis himself treaded carefully around these sensitive matters, and I have rarely heard questions on the compatibility of Islamic law and human rights raised by either Christians or Muslims in the country.

The final issue raised by Khamis related to the judicial role of the Kadhis courts, a point that was also raised by Wandati. As mentioned earlier, Khamis expanded on the recommendations heard by the Kenya Constitutional Review Commission. These recommendations seem to bring up the entanglement of religious and judicial matters, some of which needed to be separated, according to Khamis. Muslims of Kenya recommended that the appointment of kadhis should be clarified and the qualification requirements for a kadhi, particularly chief kadhi, be raised. At the time, kadhis were appointed by a Judicial Services Commission that seemed an anomaly to Khamis. He framed this situation in a rhetorical question: "Muslims as I said have held the chief kadhi to be a spiritual leader at one time and a judicial officer at another time, so if he is going to be a spiritual leader, what role should the government have in appointing that spiritual leader?" This is an important question that can be equally directed at Muslims. Like Wandati, Khamis believed that some of the functions performed by the current chief kadhi, like the confirmation of the sighting of the moon for Kenyans at the end of Ramadan, were no longer appropriate for a kadhi. Both Wandati and Khamis were admitting that the kadhis' authority within Muslim communities was not unchallenged. As with the Supreme Council of Kenya Muslims, the kadhis were challenged by new religious leaders and ordinary Kenyan Muslims. Their solution to this problem was a proposal to distinguish between judicial and religious matters.

In summary, then, Khamis presented the perspective of a Muslim legal professional. He too was grappling with the viability of an Islamic state like Wandati and Slatch, and tended to prefer a secular state in the face of an ascendant Christian church. Kadhis courts served only Muslims, but Khamis was also calling for some changes to the laws affecting Muslim personal relations. Moreover, according to Khamis, the development of Kenya society, and the impact of modernization as evidence in the sighting of the moon, called for a differentiated approach within the public sector. Kadhis should be only be concerned about judicial matters, leaving issues of religion to public leaders. They were not as clear as to who the latter should be, as they also seemed to reject the Supreme Council of Kenya Muslims.

Islamic Legal Reform and Public Sphere Competition

I turn now to Chief Kadhi Hammad, whom I first met in Mombasa in 2003.[16] Kadhi Hammad had recently taken on the position, after having served as a kadhi for about ten years. He conducted most of his studies in Kenya, mainly with his father Muhammad Qasim, who was Kenya's chief kadhi from 1963 to 1968. He was then sent to Iraq for further studies, but studied physics there instead of Islamic law. He was struck by the low prestige afforded to Islamic sciences in the country, in comparison with East Africa. He had to leave Iraq because of the outbreak of the Iran-Iraq war, and then turned to Saudi Arabia where he completed a degree in science education. He finally completed a master's degree in Islamic law in Nigeria, at the Ahmadu Bello University in Zaria.

The kadhi reflected mostly on the required reforms in the Kadhis courts, revealing both the strengths and weaknesses of the existing system. These reforms also turned to the relationship between Islamic law and Kenya's national laws. He then turned to the public perception of Kadhis courts, divided between Christian opposition and growing Muslim support.

[16] Kadhi Hammad, interview with A. I. Tayob, Mombasa, June 6, 2003.

Kadhi Hammad opened the interview by supporting the development of rulings within Islamic law that would support victims of the AIDS virus. He commented on cultural practices among Muslims in Kenya that made women and children particularly vulnerable:

> AIDS is a very serious problem among the Muslims. And what pains me a lot is that many of the victims are innocent.
>
> And what pains me even more is that because of . . . traditions that we have, of usually pointing fingers at the women . . . mostly it is the women who are accused.

The kadhi seemed to echo the sentiments of Khamis with regard to the rights of women in society. The usual response to the HIV and AIDS pandemic was to focus on sexual promiscuity in society, particularly on women's promiscuity. In the kadhi's words, Muslims "still insist that it is *zinaa, zinaa, zinaa* [sexual promiscuity] that causes it." Kadhi Hammad wanted to train other kadhis to be attentive to the harm caused to the innocent. For Kadhi Hammad, this was not a complicated matter within Islamic law. The legal principle of injury (*ḍarar*) could be expanded quite easily to apply to cases of AIDS infection. There were also cases in the practice of Islamic law where the tradition was silent, and which also needed to be updated and changed. Thus, Kadhi Hammad appealed to his colleagues for taking into consideration the rights of children as clarified in this quotation:

> A kadhi in Lamu made the ruling of such a nature, where he allowed the woman to give away her infant child, in exchange for a house. So things which are there sometimes in . . . books, but these books have been written or the scholars who have been commenting on such issues lived . . . a hundred years [ago, when] there were no discretions about rights of children also . . . the father might be having these rights, the mother might be having these rights, but the child also has rights, has rights also. Will the child really be better off in the hands of the father than in the hands of the mother?

Kadhi Hammad's views are in line with major modern reformist scholars of Islamic law who favor the adaptation and even development of Islamic juristic rulings in contemporary society.

The kadhi reflected also on the need for a better appointments system for judges. However, he did not see the need for Muslims to sit on the Judicial Service Commission, as many other Muslims had asked. He thought that the interview process for new kadhis was far too simplistic, and did not provide a sound basis for evaluating the qualifications of a kadhi. He also did not see the need for further legal training of the kadhis. He admitted, however, that Kadhis courts were not following procedures in a systematic and consistent manner, often leading to grave injustices. The following quotes illustrate Kadhi Hammad's train of thought on training in procedure, adopting procedure from Kenyan law and serving the ends of justice:

> I believe they should be trained in the civil procedure. Because the civil procedure is the tool that is used now to, to file cases, evidence . . . and most of the things agreed totally with . . . Islamic law.
>
> Islamic law might not be talking a lot about those things, but we as Muslim scholars, we can also come up with those things which agree . . . with Islamic law.
>
> The kadhi himself also should be . . . well trained so that something should not happen that is unjustified according to the procedure, and it ends up with somebody losing his rights . . .

In his view, judicial procedure was open to development and adaptation. In many respects, then, the kadhi was supportive of measures to improve the system by adopting values and measures in modern legal thought, and incorporating them in the practices of the Kadhis courts. The ends of justice for Kadhi Hammad were most important.

The kadhi, however, did not see the full convergence of the Kadhis courts into the judicial system of Kenya. This can be seen on his views on one particular recommendation proposed to the Kenya Constitutional Review Commission that received a lot of attention in public debate. The commission heard recommendations to introduce an appeals process within the Kadhis courts. Cases at local Kadhi courts should be heard by higher Kadhis courts. The current system did not allow a second hearing in the Kadhis courts; appeals were heard in the higher national courts. Kadhi Hammad was concerned that the lack of an appeal process did not allow judicial pluralism of Islamic law to work efficiently. Litigants who lost their cases in Kadhis courts were forced take their appeals to a court where the full impact and implications of Islamic law were not considered. Moreover, the Kadhis courts were not able to develop and address problems:

> The people have themselves agreed that they are Muslims and they want to be judged Islamically, then there should be no allowance to go and be heard by another law just because he lost the case in the first. He should be heard again by another Islamic court that will see to it whether the kadhi really did [make] a mistake. It could be that he made a mistake, it could be that he did not consider part of the evidence that was given, it could be that he was biased, it could be that he was corrupt, you know there are so many things that could happen.

This was a hypothetical example, but seems to reveal some of the problems that the chief kadhi recognized in the application of Islamic law in Kenya. It revealed the challenges facing Kadhis courts which people like Khamis and other Muslims expressed during the hearings and in my interviews. Muslims in Kenya were almost unanimous in asking for reforms within the Kadhi system. Kadhi Hammad also supported reforms, but believed that the problems could be addressed within the system.

This last point to be raised from his interview was also related to his view on the interface between Islamic law as applied in the Kadhis courts and Kenyan national law. The kadhi was clearly supportive and open to the impact of new ethical challenges to Islamic law. The example of children's rights and the rights of people living with AIDS mentioned above make this very clear. However, he was clear that the distinctiveness of Kadhis courts from other courts should be maintained:

> We believe that if somebody is appointed as a kadhi he should only be [a kadhi] of Islam. You know it shouldn't be that he wears one hat at one time then wears another hat at another time.

The kadhi was opposed to the training of kadhis in both Islamic and secular legal systems. He was particularly insistent that Muslims coming to the court should be able to make a distinction between Islamic and national laws. Commenting on a case where kadhis were asked to judge cases in Kenyan law, he referred particularly to its impact on Muslims: "And the Muslims said that they had no confidence with these kadhis anymore, because they were hearing cases that were un-Islamic [national laws] so it means that they believed in these other laws also to be applicable even to the Muslims." The kadhi wanted to maintain the identity and distinction between the Kadhis courts and the national court system. The two should not be associated with each other. This comment raises an important question about the public debate. One of the main objections to the Kadhis courts by some Christians was their place within the national judiciary. The chief kadhi was himself keen on keeping national and Kadhis courts as clearly separate from each other as possible. His comment also pointed to a deeper challenge of Kadhis courts and Islamic law in relation to national laws. According to the kadhis, these laws were "un-Islamic" and ought not to be believed in by Muslims. In this short quote, it would appear that the application of personal law in Kadhis courts might be creating a particular attitude towards national laws. While focusing on personal law, Kadhis courts were perhaps alienating Muslims from other laws.

This last point is clearly related to national and religious identities raised by Khamis, Slatch, and Wandati. The chief kadhi's reflection on the polarization between Muslims and Christians in the public sphere was also significant. According to him, Christians were afraid of the growing presence of Islam in Kenya: "I visited Nairobi twenty years ago, you could hardly find a woman in *hijab* [Islamic dress for women], but now it's the opposite." This presence of the *hijab* reflected a general Islamic revival globally, but it was supported by the desire of Kenyans who "find Islam to be more agreeable to their own traditions and customs." The kadhi was alluding to increased awareness among Kenyan Muslims to turn to Islam, alluding also to conversion among Kenyans to Islam. According to the kadhi, the agitation against the Kadhis courts by Christians was an attempt to undermine the national profile of Islam in Kenya. Since Christians were equally enthusiastic about conversions, they saw the Kadhis courts as a victory for Muslims on a symbolic level. Kadhi Hammad, then, could appreciate the concern of Christians from the perspective that both groups competed with each other in the public sphere of Kenya.

Kadhi Hammad, then, presented a perspective on Kadhis courts that seemed to go in two directions. On the one hand, reforms in Kadhis courts were vital to take into consideration changing mores and values. These could be developed within Islamic law, or they could be drawn from general ethical and legal considerations. There were also other more technical areas that needed attention in the Kadhis courts. On the other hand, the kadhi favored a clear separation of the systems of Kadhis courts and national courts. Apart from preserving the integrity of Kadhis courts, Kadhi Hammad also recognized and endorsed an inevitable competition between Muslims and Christian within public life.

Discussion and Conclusion

The interviews very clearly reflect some Kenyan Muslim positions on the general nature of the state, the place of Muslims therein, and the particular role and function of the Kadhis courts. It seems that the politics of accommodation that Haynes and Constantin documented during the postcolonial period was being replaced by a different kind of politics. The formation of the Islamic Party in 1992 was a first attempt to produce a new politics, but the Kadhis courts controversy provided an opportunity to rethink and offer a different approach. Using the three major themes of the interviews, I offer some reflections on the kind of politics proposed and reflected upon by my interviewees.

The first issue relates to the nature of the state. There was an automatic reflex view from the interviewees about the political goal of Muslims. This was illustrated very well by Khamis's first reaction that he would preferably like to live in an Islamic state. One may assume that Wandati in 1992 when he founded the Islamic Party may have had similar hopes. Khamis turned away from his initial response, however, and deliberated on the value of a secular option on the basis of practical considerations, and in the light of an ascendant Christian hegemony in Kenya. Similarly, Wandati was clearly taking a different perspective in his proposal for an "ecumenical" state. Oded has argued that the Islamic Party of Kenya under the leadership of Balala had been radicalized by the Kenyan police and military crackdown. Ten years later, Wandati's proposal for an ecumenical state at least indicates a deliberation on the future state for all Kenyans belonging to diverse religions.

These deliberations should be analyzed in the light of the extensive literature on Islam and the modern state. It is generally believed that Muslims would support a religious state, one in which Islamic law would be the sole and supreme source of legislation. This position was articulated and popularized by Islamists in the twentieth century like Abu al-A'la Mawdoodi (1903–1979) of the Indian subcontinent and Sayyid Qutb (1906–1966) in Egypt.[17] There are diverse opinions on this development in modern Islamic political thought. Feldman's recent study is the most hopeful that liberal and democratic values may still emerge from such a modern Islamic state, based on the balance of forces and the construction of religious values in a society. On the other extreme stand theorists

[17] H. Enayat, *Modern Islamic Political Thought* (Austin: University of Texas Press, 1982).

like Huntington for whom an Islamic state shares very little or nothing with a modern nation-state with checks and balances, let alone liberal values.[18] For Huntington, an Islamic state was no different from the pre-modern caliphate and promised a consistent and undemocratic future for Muslims. Wandati and Khamis occupy a middle position between these. Their responses suggest that they thought of an Islamic state in the first instance, but changed their positions to suit the context of Kenya. They had not yet taken the path set out by an-Naʿim who urged Muslims to adopt the secular state, and keep religion in private and public spheres.[19] However, they were clearly weighing the options of a religious state within the existing political context in Kenya, a country where some Christians desired a more religious state as well.

The particular option of an Islamic or secular state might seem pragmatic or opportunistic on the part of Muslims, but support for the separation of legal and religious spheres of Muslim practice took the political deliberations one step further. The Islamic state, as articulated in the twentieth century, was focused on the legislative authority of the shari'a in a modern state. In Kenya, in contrast, the shari'a seemed to be displaced from its central political role. The debate on Kadhis courts naturally elicited detailed responses from the kadhi and Khamis as far as Islamic law was concerned. They shared their views on the reforms necessary within Kadhis courts to maintain their ability to address the needs of litigants. The courts were clearly popular in their ability to deliver decisions and justice, but there were concerns on procedures and interpretations that did not necessarily lead to desirable results. Khamis was concerned about the judicial operations of the courts, while Kadhi Hammad reflected on the extensive reforms needed within Islamic legal thinking to address new challenges within society. The public debate had clearly suppressed both dimensions of reforms within Kadhis courts that had been brought to the attention of the review commissions. Discussions on reforms were pushed to the background as Muslims and Christians took antagonistic positions towards each other.

The activists, however, wanted a separate authority for the religious

[18] S. P. Huntington, *The Clash of Civilizations and the Remaking of the World Order* (New York: Simon and Schuster, 1996); N. Feldman, *The Fall and Rise of the Islamic State* (Princeton, N.J.: Princeton University Press, 2008).

[19] A. A. An-Naʿim, *Islam and the Secular State: Negotiating the Future of Shari'a* (Cambridge, Mass.: Harvard University Press, 2008).

symbols of Kenyan Muslims. The kadhis were recognized as state functionaries who could not represent the Muslims as part of the civic sphere. They performed a legal role, important for the adjudication of disputes in families. For Muslim politics, other forms of representations were required, like a national mufti or a national body. The interviews were critical of SUPKEM, which had been recognized by the state during the post-independent autocratic regimes. Part of their support for a new religious authority may be a response to the old politics pursued by Kenyan national Muslim representatives as discussed in Constantin's and Hayne's work cited earlier. Moreover, Khamis, Wandate, and Slatch were not clear on the boundaries of this "religious sphere," and simply fell back on a distinction between law and religion. This recognition of a distinction between law and religion is significant for the kind of politics that they were formulating. The delineation and identification of a religious sphere was an important part of how Muslims were comparing themselves with Christians, at least in this case. At least, Islam had to be represented like other religions, and a sphere with its authority needed to be identified. This distinction was an important consideration of the place of religions in the public sphere of Kenya. It was a crucial component for the future of Kenyan pluralism.

In the 1990s, Muslims and Christians made a significant contribution to pressure the Moi government to review the constitution. However, there was a third dimension of Muslim politics that should be included in this review. Both Christians and Muslims invested considerable energies into competing with each other on the symbolic role occupied by the other. Given the desire to infuse the public space with their own symbols, Christians could not cooperate with Muslims who were not prepared to compromise on Kadhis courts. Slatch and Wandati watched with horror as political meetings were turned into Christian prayer meetings. But this competition was clearly also revealed on the Muslim side. Kadhi Hammad revealed some of the spirit with which Muslims saw the revival of Islamic practices in Kenya. With a deep sense of satisfaction, Muslim symbols were read triumphantly. Leaders of religious communities strove to make their symbols dominant in the public sphere. The reason for such a competition may have been for the battle over conversions in the country. More generally, for the public sphere, it was a desire to see the public sphere completely taken over by the images and symbols of one's own religion. Whilst Muslims and Christians may continue to make a constructive contribution to public life, their efforts may also be limited by their desire to see their respective symbols dominate the public sphere.

One can, then, speak about a new politics being deliberated among Muslims during the controversy over the place of Kadhis courts in Kenya. While Christian and Muslim religious leaders exchanged statements on their validity in the constitution of a pluralist state, Muslims were reflecting on the future of Muslim politics in the country. From my interviews, I have identified three major deliberations. First, there was a consideration on the nature of the Kenyan state. Presented by a dominant construction of an Islamic state, some Kenyan Muslims were thinking of different options like an ecumenical or secular state. Second, and more importantly, they also were making a distinction between legal and religious spheres. This distinction was important for the search for a religious authority that occupied the public sphere. And third, Muslims saw the public space as an arena of competition and not always of cooperation with Christians.

Works Cited

An-Naʿim, Abdullahi Ahmed, *Islam and the Secular State: Negotiating the Future of Shariʿa* (Cambridge, Mass.: Harvard University Press, 2008).

Chesworth, John A., "Kadhi's Courts in Kenya: Reactions and Responses," in *Constitutional Review in Kenya and Kadhis Courts: Selected Papers Presented at the Workshop 20 March 2010*, ed. Abdulkader Tayob and Joseph Wandera (Cape Town: Centre for Contemporary Islam, 2011).

Constantin, François, "Charisma and the Crisis of Power in East Africa," in *Charisma and Brotherhood in African Islam*, ed. Donal B. Cruise O'Brien and Christian Coulon (Oxford: Clarendon, 1988).

———, "Leadership, Muslim Identities, and East African Politics: Tradition, Bureaucratisation and Communication," in *Muslim Identity and Social Change in Sub-Saharan Africa*, ed. Louis Brenner (London: Hurst, 1993).

———, "Muslims and Politics: The Attempts to Create Muslim National Organisations in Tanzania, Uganda and Kenya," in *Religion and Politics in East Africa: The Period Since Independence*, ed. Holger Bernt Hansen and Michael Twaddle (London: James Curry, 1995).

Cussac, Anne, "Muslims and Politics in Kenya: The Issue of the Kadhis' Courts in the Constitution Review Process," *Journal of Muslim Minority Affairs* 28, no. 2 (2008): 289–302.

Enayat, Hamid, *Modern Islamic Political Thought* (Austin: University of Texas Press, 1982).

Feldman, Noah, *The Fall and Rise of the Islamic State* (Princeton, N.J.: Princeton University Press, 2008).

Hassan, Ahmed Issack (Commissioner), "Working Document for the Constitution of Kenya Review Commission on the Kadhi's Courts, Chief Kadhi and Kadhis," http://www.kenyaconstitution.org/docs/07d046.htm.

Haynes, Jeffrey, "Islam and Democracy in East Africa," *Democratization* 13, no. 3 (2006): 490–507.

Huntington, Samuel P., *The Clash of Civilizations and the Remaking of the World Order* (New York: Simon and Schuster, 1996).

Kresse, Kai, "Muslim Politics in Postcolonial Kenya: Negotiating Knowledge on the Double-Periphery," *Journal of the Royal Anthropological Institute* 15 (2009): 76–94.

Maina, Kahumbi, "Islamophobia Among Christians and Its Challenges in Entrenchment of Kadhis Courts in Kenya," in *Constitutional Review in Kenya and Kadhis Courts: Selected Papers Presented at the Workshop 20 March 2010*, ed. Abdulkader Tayob and Joseph Wandera (Cape Town: Centre for Contemporary Islam, 2011).

Mazrui, Alamin, "Ethnicity and Pluralism: The Politicization of Religion in Kenya," *Journal of Muslim Minority Affairs* 14, no. 1 (1993): 191–201.

Oded, Arye, "Islamic Extremism in Kenya: The Rise and Fall of Sheikh Khalid Balala," *Journal of Religion in Africa* 26, no. 4 (1996): 406–15.

———, *Islam and Politics in Kenya* (London: Lynne Rienner, 2000).

"Recommendations to the Constitution of Kenya Review Commission on the Proposed Draft Constitution of the Republic of Kenya," *The Kenya Church* (2002).

Tayob, Abdulkader I., "The Demand for Sharīʿah in African Democratisation Processes: Pitfalls or Opportunities?" in *Comparative Perspectives on Shari'ah in Nigeria*, ed. Philip Ostien et al. (Ibadan: Spectrum Books, 2005).

Wandera, Joseph, "Anglican Responses to Kadhis Courts in Kenya," in *Constitutional Review in Kenya and Kadhis Courts: Selected Papers Presented at the Workshop 20 March 2010*, ed. Abdulkader Tayob and Joseph Wandera (Cape Town: Centre for Contemporary Islam, 2011).

BOOK REVIEWS

DOI: 10.5192/215409930401125

Ousmane Kane. *The Homeland Is the Arena: Religion, Transnationalism, and the Integration of Senegalese Immigrants in America.* New York: Oxford University Press, 2011. Pp. xvi + 311. $99.00, hardback (ISBN 0-19-973230-2); $35.00, paperback (ISBN 0-19-973231-9).

In *The Homeland Is the Arena*, Ousmane Kane highlights the importance of religion, specifically Islam, to advancing studies of migration and transnationalism. He seeks to understand how migration abroad shapes Muslim thought and practice in Senegal as well as how the presence of Senegalese in America contributes to Muslim practice and perceptions of Muslims in this country. In fact, as he argues, there is now more than ever a need for scholarly work on Muslims in the West. Furthermore, as Africa has shifted to become what some would call the new front line on terror, Kane's book takes on increasing relevance in the world today. This work contributes to a growing literature on Islam in West Africa. It does so notably by including the voices and experiences of migrant women as much as those of migrant men. His work engages with scholarly debates about Islam in Senegal, including the nature of spiritual authority, and at the same time provides a much-needed focus on the everyday lives and struggles of ordinary Muslims.

In general, Kane's field-based research in the United States focuses on Muslim associations in New York City, including Harlem, Brooklyn, and the Bronx. Part 1 of the book focuses on the development of Sufi congregations in the colonial period and their relations with the state in the post-colonial period. Kane's analysis focuses for the most part on Murid and Tijani Sufi congregations. Part 1 provides an accessible introduction to Muslim thought and practice in West Africa and at the same time provides sufficient depth and complexity of argument to interest specialists on the subject.

As a classic case study in migration, part 2 of the book focuses on the integration of Senegalese Muslims into American society. This section is ethnographically rich and provides important, detailed studies of

Islamic Africa, VOL. 4, NO. 1, 2013. ISSN 2154-0993. www.islamicafricajournal.org.

individual lives and experiences. Part 3 of the book focuses on building networks with those at home, in Senegal. Here Kane focuses on the development of a transnational spiritual economy involving a circuit of shaykhs moving between Senegal and Senegalese migrants abroad.

Kane shows the fraught nature of "integration" as part of the mission of Senegalese associations in the United States. He demonstrates how they help migrants navigate legal, social, moral, and economic structures and strictures. Yet Kane does not question the dominant paradigm in migration studies, which is the assumption that integration is the ultimate goal. One wonders what his interlocutors think about the possibilities for integration given their experience in post-9/11 America. As Kane argues, integration into American society requires not only a desire on behalf of immigrants to integrate, but the reception of the host society. Here the ethnography could have included field-based research and policy analysis of the politics of immigration in the United States. Moreover, as the title of the book indicates, the homeland is the arena (as translated by Kane from the Wolof, *Lamb jaa nga Senegal*) in which Senegalese women and men seek to fashion their reputations and that of their families. Given the nature of circular migration between the United States and Senegal, and the continuing importance of relations with those at home, it is not clear that integration and settlement in the United States is the ultimate goal of many migrants. Kane describes in vivid detail debates between men and women concerning the allocation of family resources, the importance of the education and upbringing of children in the home country, and the changing nature of work and social support in and out of Senegal.

Beth Buggenhagen, Indiana University

Erin E. Stiles. *An Islamic Court in Context: An Ethnographic Study of Judicial Reasoning.* New York: Palgrave Macmillan, 2009. 221 pp.; glossary, bibliography, index, 1 map, 3 photographs, 5 tables. $95.00.

Scholars of Islamic law face the challenge of explaining to readers and students the array of texts, reasoning processes, and interpretation that go into this thing that we call "Islamic law" in the first place. Law, as many argue, does not exist in a vacuum in the world of text; rather, it is applied and interpreted through judges, litigants, and scholars. This is the premise of *An Islamic Court in Context*, a study of one particular Zanzibari court, and indeed, one particular kadhi, Shaykh Hamid. Based on field research conducted on the Zanzibari island of Unguja between 1999 and 2005, the book is based on Stiles's 2002 doctoral dissertation in anthropology at Washington University in St. Louis.

Chapter 1 is a strong introductory chapter which establishes the author's intervention in the literature and her methodology. Stiles engages in a useful and informed discussion of the flexibility of law, particularly Islamic law, drawing significantly on recent research in anthropology and history. Here, she underscores her main objective in writing the book: exploring the ways in which judges, clerics, and litigants understand Islamic law. In addition to this core argument, Stiles identifies two themes of discussion to be threaded through the book: an exploration of the relationship between courtroom activity and the production of written documents, and the ways in which gendered experiences of divorce and marriage influence court activity and the judges' reasoning. The situated process of judicial reasoning is most interesting to Stiles, but this does not mean discarding religious text. Instead, she perceives documentation as a product of a historical and cultural context, the result of socio-cultural engagement and intellectual reasoning based on religious and judicial precepts. The focus of this theoretical framing, Stiles tells us, will be a set of family court cases presented in the Mkokotoni court of Shaykh Hamid, a man whom Stiles clearly reveres and who sits at the center of the knowledge production outlined in the book.

Chapters 2 through 6, with a concluding assessment in chapter 7 (wonderfully titled "The Court Is a Hospital"), are largely descriptive narratives of the goings on in the Mkokotoni court, centered on the cases brought by women and men litigants and the rulings applied by Shaykh Hamid. Stiles moves back and forth between discussions of dispute framing and document production, interpretation by court staff, and gendered subject position. Stiles is at her best in chapter 4, where she explores the conceptually and practically slippery category of intention. Stiles tells readers that to some Islamic law scholars, particularly those who emphasize the power of text and discourse, intention is not so significant. However, intention is a powerful driving force, Stiles argues, and furthermore, it is measurable by culturally situated kadhis who are concerned with maintaining social harmony. Stiles shows us that there is a Shafi'i precedent for this type of legal interpretation through the fatwas of previous Zanzibari muftis. This chapter highlights the meaningful connection between the creation of text (whether text be divorce pronouncement, fatwa, or ruling) and cultural situation (intentionality and gender). The case of Mariam and Abdulmalik, which is at the center of this dispute over intent to divorce (and which appears in different moments throughout the book), highlights gendered agency at work in the vein of Susan Hirsch, Judith Tucker, Laura Fair, and Ziba Mir-Hosseini.

An Islamic Court in Context contributes new case studies to support established theoretical claims regarding the situated process of Islamic legal reasoning and the importance of attending to gender roles and performance in Islamic family courts. At times, the book reads very much like its original dissertation form, which does not serve the strength of the original contributions that Stiles is making (again, her points on intentionality are quite compelling). Stiles's arguments about the intersection of document production, gender position, and judicial reasoning could be drawn to the fore in more substantial ways throughout the chapters. The book's market price at $95.00 is near prohibitive, making it difficult to assign the monograph in classes. Still, Erin Stiles presents some useful points of analysis and observation of the situated meaning of judicial reasoning in an Islamic court, and this reader looks forward to more from Stiles in the future.

Emily Burrill, University of North Carolina at Chapel Hill

Zain Abdullah. *Black Mecca: The African Muslims of Harlem*. New York: Oxford University Press, 2010. Pp. viii, 294. $35.00

"The morning air crackles with excitement as the courtyard at the Harlem State Office Building swells with hundreds of African Muslims—men, women, and children decked out in their best *boubou* wear and headwraps. As they maneuver into position, one can still hear prayers humming with the circular motion of *thikr* beads" (107). These sentences, with which Zain Abdullah introduces the fifth chapter of *Black Mecca*, deliver a good sense of one of the main characteristics of the author's method, namely to get the reader right into the scene. In fact, reading this book is a pleasure not the least due to the thickness of its ethnography, which leads the reader directly into the streets, shops, and mosques of Harlem, those places where West African immigrants struggle in their daily lives and try to make sense of the manifold experiences resulting from their migration. Zain Abdullah's book is based to a very large extent on interviews and participant observation. Discussion of other literature on the subjects he engages with, of empirical and theoretical sorts, remains subordinate to the primary voices of the men and women who are the main protagonists of this story of migration, which is told through tropes of loss, diaspora, and exile, but also tropes of reinvention, arrival, and emancipation.

The book is organized in nine chapters (including prologue and epilogue) and also contains a glossary, which is helpful in particular for those readers not acquainted with Islamic terms, as well as a very detailed index. Relating and integrating the experiences of recent Muslim West African immigrants to Harlem into the larger history of black peoples in America, the author suggests understanding the former as another "Blues People" (a notion attributed to LeRoi Jones): "For me, the blues is a metaphor. It is a way to begin a conversation about the sensibilities of a people—their dreams, fears, and hopes" (5). The main chapters are structured thematically, focusing on what Abdullah identifies as central issues shaping the lifeworlds of Muslim West African immigrants to Harlem. This story necessarily begins with the drama of migration itself, which is brought to us most comprehensively in chapter 2 ("America Dreaming"). Here and elsewhere in the book it is the very immediacy provided by the personal access to these experiences that is gripping and convincing in both rational and emotional ways. The story we are told dialectically connects the severe economic conditions in the migrants' home countries with the utopia of an American paradise, providing insight into the—for many—traumatic experiences of migration and fleshing out the clash of expectations and frustrations after arrival. In a way this book can be read as an anthropological micro-study on the dislocations that accompany processes of economic and social globalization.

Chapter 3 ("The Black Encounter") is one of the most intriguing parts of the book. Skillfully leading us through prearranged as well as spontaneous conversations with African migrants and local African Americans, Abdullah provides a view of the complexity of their encounter in Harlem/United States. This is an encounter shaped by socioeconomic fears and competition, problems of communication based on cultural differences (food, clothing, music, body language, etc.) and misunderstandings, as well as language issues (language is also the focus of chapter 4), differing notions of race, blackness, and Africanness, and lastly very different views on America as a reality and as a promise. The major focus is thereby on matters of identity and belonging. Some of the questions addressed here and throughout are: "When does Islam matter, and when is it a non-issue? When does race matter? And when and in what ways is an African sense of self important? In sum, how do West African Muslims imagine themselves and their life with others in Harlem?" (60).

While the relationship between West African immigrants, the overwhelming majority of whom are Muslim, and their predominantly black environment in Harlem seems to be dominated by mutual suspicion and animosities, Abdullah also presents us with more optimistic voices, which articulate notions of racial and religious commonality as important cornerstones on which solidarity and brotherhood could be built. This hope seems to be particularly pronounced when it comes to alliances between African and African American co-religionists—even if, as this book illustrates in manifold ways, the forms of Islam found within both groups are themselves anything but monolithic (70–71). The more ethnic and/or Sufi-imbued forms of Islam practiced by many West African Muslims bear potential for conflict with the forms of Islam dominant among African American Muslims, who mostly associate with legalist forms of Sunnism critical of ethnic particularisms and Sufi practices, or who subscribe to racialist readings of Islam in the tradition of the Nation of Islam (130–41).

The role of religion in the West African Muslims' story of migration is one major focus of *Black Mecca*. As Abdullah shows convincingly, their Islam helps them to make sense of the migration experience itself, as well as of social and economic hardships and suffering in the American diaspora. It provides social networks that to a certain extent substitute for extended family networks back home (addressed in chapter 8, "Family Matters"). Religion can also be a means to endure and reenergize, as well as a source for ethical standards in contexts in which traditional norms clash with the foreign norms and values of (black) America.

The Senegalese Murid Sufi order, which has a prominent place in Muslim Harlem, is the group that receives the most attention in *Black Mecca*. Chapter 5 ("A Sacred City") takes the Murids' annual Ahmadu Bamba Day celebration as a starting point for discussing how African Muslim migrants incorporate Harlem America through various kinds of practices (marching, chanting, display of pictures) into their religioscape. This incorporation is accomplished in ways that reflect how the Murids adjust and connect to black American sensibilities. The patron saint of the Murid order, Ahmadu Bamba, for example, is in this context presented in a way that unites his anti-colonialist quest with notions of black empowerment, civil rights, and anti-racism (111–13). One of the major achievements of Abdullah's study is to develop an intricate understanding of how the African-black encounter triggers reflection and rethinking of preconceived notions of religion, race, Africanness, and blackness on both sides. But the Ahmadu Bamba Day celebrations also show how the primary other for West African immigrants of Harlem remains the broader U.S. society, reflected in the prominent display of American flags, and in rhetoric that draws positively on "American" themes—highly important for a Muslim community in the United States in post-9/11 times (115–16).

Chapter 6 ("Harlem Jihads") is organized around the concept of religious struggle (jihad) as a way to explain how West African Muslims in Harlem draw on religion as an ethics and a worldview that helps them manage and rationalize their daily battles and frustrations in their Harlem diaspora. The chapter also links the West African Muslims' Harlem experiences to broader socioeconomic developments and in particular the force of gentrification. Chapter 7 ("Doing Allah's Work") interrogates the role of Islam in migrants' efforts to cope with and rationalize the often brutal conditions of working and living in the United States as recent African Muslim immigrants, often illegal. Here, the author employs the Islamic concept of *'amal saalih*, "righteous work," which he uses to discuss the various ways in which his protagonists interpret the quest of being economically successful without going against the religion.

Putting religion at the center of an analysis of complex social phenomena always bears the temptation of overemphasizing its role in the explanation of complex realities, and the multitude of values, motivations, and worldviews of social actors. One might criticize that Abdullah, though in principle very careful to represent the lives of West Africans in Harlem as impacted by a variety of social factors, not the least socioeconomic pressures and considerations, at times succumbs to this temptation. An example of that would be the prominent role that he attributes to Islam as a means for West African Muslim migrants "to make sense" of their experiences in the new Harlem lands (87).

In conclusion, *Black Mecca* is a masterful example of thick ethnography, which generates a remarkable feeling of intimacy. Despite being written with much empathy, however, Abdullah never betrays his critical stance and achieves a fluid connection between inside and outside perspectives on the lives and lifeworlds of his protagonists. I only detected a few typos and errors, for example, the Arabic concept of "God consciousness" is *taqwa*, not *taqiyya* (which means legitimate religious disguise) (126).

I strongly recommend this book as an ethnographic study that combines great storytelling with deep insights into the complex semantics of identity construction among African and black communities in the United

States and will certainly be very well received within the fields of black and African diaspora studies. The book is a must read for students of American Islam, and is highly recommended for students of migration with an interest in the role of religion/Islam therein.

Markus Dressler, Istanbul Technical University

Rüdiger Seesemann. *The Divine Flood: Ibrahim Niasse and the Roots of a Twentieth-Century Sufi Revival.* New York: Oxford University Press, 2011. Pp. 331 + xii. $65.00.

In *The Divine Flood*, Rüdiger Seesemann provides a richly detailed and theoretically shrewd study of the life and writings of the Senegalese Sufi Ibrahim Niasse (1900–1975) and the spread across West Africa of the community he founded. The focus is at once on the Jamaᶜat al-Fayda ("Community of the Divine Flood") that Niasse established in 1929 and the distinct spiritual method that he articulated in his writings, a method which set the community apart from its many religious competitors in the region. Seesemann's analysis is built on an extremely wide primary source base in Arabic and other African languages that ranges from earlier Tijani classics to the treatises, letters, poems, and travelogues written by Niasse and his followers; French colonial archives provide context from outside the tradition. Seesemann uses these materials to carefully reconstruct the dynamics of socio-religious connection between Senegal, Gambia, Mauritania, Sudan, and northern Nigeria between the 1920s and 1950s. This was the period that marked the first, African phase of Jamaᶜat al-Fayda expansion prior to its second phase of expansion beyond Africa, with which *The Divine Flood* does not deal in detail.

Much of the focus is on the founder, Ibrahim Niasse, who was born into a respected scholarly and Sufi family, albeit one belonging (according to his detractors) to the low-status blacksmith caste. Niasse was introduced to the Tijaniyya by his own father, who had himself previously traveled to Mauritania, Morocco, Marseilles, and the Hijaz. The key year in Niasse's career was 1929 when, having acquired multiple Sufi initiations during his early manhood in the 1920s, he underwent the transformative mystical experience of the "divine flood" (*fayda*) and in response founded the new Sufi organization of the Jamaᶜat al-Fayda. By 1934, the first hagiography of Ibrahim Niasse was written, marking his transformation into a living saint and forming one of the major discursive steps towards his success. In the five chapters of his book, Seesemann works through this extensive and rhetorically complex body of writings that emerged around Niasse, comprising both his own writings and those of his followers and colonial observers. The chapters focus respectively on Niasse's early life; the evolution of his teachings (particularly as expressed in his highly influential 1931 *Kashif al-Ilbas*); the foundation of the "Community of the Divine Flood"; the first decades of its spread across West Africa; and the midlife years in which Niasse's claims won recognition. Chapter 5 is especially fascinating in its use of the verse travelogues written by Niasse in the 1930s and 1940s to trace the early transnational expansion of the Jamaʿat al-Fayda via the peregrinations of its founder. Through an effective critical reading of these works, Seesemann is able not merely to trace Niasse's movements, but to show how these journeys were made meaningful by Niasse himself and articulated in turn to his audiences.

What is most notable about Seesemann's method is his ability to situate Niasse in the vertical diachronic context of the Sufi Muslim tradition in which Niasse and his followers situated themselves. By drawing on earlier texts in the Tijani tradition in a sophisticated and critical hermeneutics, the author is able to show how Niasse both drew on and differed from his predecessors. These distinctions are crucial for making sense of the rhetoric and success of the Jamaʿat al-Fayda through its claim of presenting an improved *tarbiya* or training method for accessing experiential knowledge of the divine realms. The presentation of an African Muslim sense of (and use of) tradition and history is particularly fascinating for showing how Niasse was able to present himself as the "bringer of the flood" prophesied by the great Ahmad al-Tijani more than a century earlier. Not only does Seesemann locate these African actors in their own historical schemata, he also takes seriously the agency of their religious moves. Indeed, while the rise of the Jama'at al-Fayda is situated in the familiar sociopolitical context of the Western historian, Seesemann's main focus is on Niasse's training method, which he argues was the key agent in the Jamaʿat al-Fayda's appeal and success.

In this way, *The Divine Flood* is best regarded as a study in and of a tradition, of the processes of rumination, reinterpretation, and renewal of a Tijani legacy that is revealed as a potent and flexible resource in the mid-century decades of colonial rule and decolonization. The book is tremendously effective in unveiling the sophistication and dynamism of an African Islamic tradition at the height of a colonial period in which such knowledge was routinely denigrated. But as a consequence of locating Niasse and his followers most fully in their "own" terms—particularly in the vertical and intertextual tradition of Tijani writings—*The Divine Flood* is much stronger on the texts than their contexts. Seesemann does effectively handle such contextualization with regard to the organization and spread of the Jamaʿat al-Fayda, especially on the question of why it was more successful outside of Niasse's Senegalese homeland and on the use of transnational matrimonial alliances. But while there are many detailed analytical summaries of Jamaʿat al-Fayda writings, in chapters 2 and 3 especially there is relatively little attempt to link the *doctrines* that emerge from the textual analysis with their fuller contexts beyond the Tijani tradition. Given the author's argument that Niasse's method (*tarbiya*) was the crucial factor in his success—that "his method of spiritual training . . . triggered the large-scale expansion of the Tijāniyya" (225)—the case would have succeeded better with a fuller demonstration of how this method interacted with the sociopolitical setting or other, perhaps more immediate and existential concerns, of his followers. While it is undoubtedly a difficult task, the linking of spiritual doctrine with concrete context remains one of the largest lacunae in Islamic studies. On a larger contextual scale, other immediate questions also remain unanswered—such as how the Jamaʿat al-Fayda should be compared with the contemporaneous rise of the Tariqat al-Muridiyya (Murids) and what the rise of both organizations tells us about late colonial and decolonizing West African societies more generally.

However, these more mundane and perhaps over-familiar historical questions are not those which *The Divine Flood* primarily sets out to address. For in conceiving the founder and members of the Jamaʿat al-Fayda as "people who had genuine religious experiences," the author draws on a huge reservoir of primary texts to show how African Muslims "saw the events unfolding during and after the emergence of the divine flood [in 1929/30] through the lens of their religious worldview" (229). This is, then, an approach that "values the ideas and experiences of the practitioners and elucidates their religious world" (230) and on these—its own—terms the book succeeds impressively. With remarkable erudition and methodological astuteness, Rüdiger Seesemann has written a landmark study of a major African religious movement that contributes as much to African intellectual history as it does to the history of Sufism.

Nile Green, University of California, Los Angeles